METHODICAL REALISM

ÉTIENNE GILSON

Methodical Realism

A Handbook for Beginning Realists

Translated by
Philip Trower

IGNATIUS PRESS   SAN FRANCISCO

Original French edition:
Le réalisme méthodique
© 1935 by Pierre Téqui *éditeur*, Paris

English translation:
© 1990 by Christendom Press, Front Royal, Virginia

Cover photograph
© Rick J/iStockphoto

Cover design by Roxanne Mei Lum

Published in 2011 by Ignatius Press, San Francisco
ISBN 978-1-58617-304-3
Library of Congress Control Number 2010931308
Printed in the United States of America ∞

CONTENTS

To My Friend

The Reverend Dr. G. B. Phelan

Director of the Institute of Medieval Studies
Toronto, Canada

It is not certain, it is not at any rate demonstrated, that what is neglected by the very nature of the method is in fact negligible.

—Léon Brunschvicg

The essays that follow and most of which have already appeared in various journals are gathered here only to defer to a wish conveyed to me by Mr. Yves Simon. May he allow me to express my gratitude and also to share with him in the responsibility, not for the ideas contained in these essays, but for a publication of which, without him, I would not have thought.

É. G.

I

Methodical Realism

The overriding importance of the problem of knowledge in modern philosophies is plain enough. But there is something which is perhaps not so easily noticed: that to some extent even neo-scholasticism is affected by the preoccupation with epistemology. Yet it is a fact.

What the opponents of the scholastic tradition blame it for—when they condescend to concern themselves with it—is either not being a philosophy at all because tainted by its connections with theology, or being a dogmatic and naïve realism which has no idea at all what critical idealism is and which has stopped short at the threshold of true philosophy. As a result, this opposition has provoked the champions of the *philosophia perennis* into criticizing critical philosophy and into trying to show that at bottom their system alone is capable of bringing to the problems raised by idealism the solutions they call for.

What do the systems which the neo-scholastic philosophers want to refute have in common? The idea that philosophical reflection ought necessarily to go from thought to things. The mathematician always proceeds from thought to being or things. Consequently, critical idealism was born the day Descartes decided that the mathematical method must henceforth be the method for metaphysics. Reversing the method of Aristotle and the medieval tradition, Descartes decided that *a nosse ad esse valet consequential* [it is valid to infer being from knowing], to which he added that this was indeed the only valid type of inference, so that in his philosophy whatever can be clearly and distinctly attributed to the idea of the thing is true of the thing itself: *cum quid dicimus in alicujus rei natura, sive conceptu, contineri, idem est ac si diceremus id de ea re verum esse, sive de ipsa posse affirmari.* [When we say of anything that it is contained in the nature or concept of a particular thing, it is the same as if we were to say it is true of that thing, or could be affirmed of it]. This in fact was where the Copernican revolution in philosophy took place for the first time.

That Descartes, although an idealist in method, was in intention a realist, is proved by his *Meditations on First Philosophy*. We can also say that in asking himself under what conditions a universal a priori mathematics is possible, he still left the door open for metaphysics as a genuine science. But when Kant carried the Cartesian method onto other ground and asked himself what are the conditions which make Newtonian physics possible, he firmly shut the door on metaphysics as a science, because all physics presupposes sensory intuition, which is plainly not to be found in the metaphysical ideas of the reason. Indeed, all idealism derives from Descartes, or from Kant, or from both together, and whatever other distinguishing features a system may have, it is idealist to the extent that, either in itself, or as far as we are concerned, it makes knowing the condition of being.

It is, therefore, quite natural that neo-scholastic philosophers should be anxious to re-establish the lawfulness of the traditional point of view. They cannot fail to feel the need to, because the impression of meeting something old-fashioned, which a reader has when turning from any modern system of philosophy to any scholastic system, derives precisely from the fact that the three centuries of

philosophical speculation which have intervened between
the scholastic period and the present have made us lose the
habit, and even forget the possibility, of thinking from the
perspective of the object.

Needless to say it is not easy to go back and make a fresh
start, if we stop short of Descartes. With Descartes the *Cogito
ergo sum* [I think, therefore I am] turns into *Cogito ergo res sunt*
[I think, therefore things are]. But alerted as we are by the
speculations of Malebranche and Hume, we feel more keenly
the difficulty of getting outside the knowing subject to the
object known. That is why the philosopher who tries to justify the traditional position immediately feels the need to show
that thought is not imprisoned in itself, but either reaches or
implies the object. And that is what certain neo-scholastics
call refuting idealism. It is insofar as they succeed, or think
they have succeeded, that they consider themselves realists.
The transition from here to becoming interested in every man-
ifestation of neo-realism in contemporary thought is a natural one; neo-realism, to the extent that it is an effective weapon
against idealism, is an ally for neo-scholasticism. This is why
it is today taken for granted that all scholastic philosophy is
realist, and all neo-scholastic philosophy neo-realist, that they
are such by definition. But in what sense are they?

The fact is the business is not as simple as it looks—and
the variety of solutions offered makes this only the more
evident. Put in the simplest terms, the question comes down
to what has been called "the problem of the bridge". As L.
Noël has clearly shown in his penetrating *Notes d'épistémologie
thomiste*,[1] the problem thus conceived is the result of pic-
turing things in spatial terms. The object is placed on one
side, the understanding on the other, and the question is
then asked how the object can be where it is while at the

---

[1] L. Noël, *Notes d'epistémologie thomiste* (Louvain-Paris, 1925), p. 33.

same time being somewhere else, that is to say—as some people put it—*inside* consciousness; or how consciousness, while remaining itself, can depart from itself to lodge *in* the object. Furthermore, as L. Noël has also stated in a definitive manner, thought gets beyond this naïvely imaginative stage only to find itself in an impasse, because one can only cross a bridge which exists, and here there is none. A thought which starts from a mental representation will never get beyond it:

> From the duplicate or image there is no way of reaching the thing itself. Once trapped in immanence, the duplicate is only a mental symbol and will remain such. The principle of causality does not in the least change the situation. If you have a hook painted on a wall, the only thing you will ever be able to hang from it is a chain also painted on the wall. Belief and dogmatic assertion will help us even less; as essentially interior acts, they cannot get us out of our prison either. (p. 73)

In other words, he who begins as an idealist ends as an idealist; one cannot safely make a concession or two to idealism here and there. One might have suspected as much, since history is there to teach us on this point. *Cogito ergo res sunt* is pure Cartesianism, that is to say, the exact antithesis of what is thought of as scholastic realism and the cause of its ruin. Nobody has tried as hard as Descartes to build a bridge from thought to things, by relying on the principle of causality. He was also the first to make the attempt, and he did so because he was forced to by having set the starting point for knowledge in the intuition of thought. It is, therefore, strictly true that every scholastic who thinks himself a realist, because he accepts this way of stating the problem, is in fact a Cartesian.

With even more reason is such a scholastic a Cartesian if he makes the first step in his process of deduction the immediate perception of being as found in the thinking subject. As we know, this position too has been taken. In studying *Le problème critique fondamental*, we find that S. Picard keeps returning to an attitude very close to that of Descartes. "What allows me", he says, "to maintain that I grasp in myself in an absolute way the absolute nature of being is that I grasp myself as existing: I am. In this simple 'I am' I have the absolute datum of being, namely, that it exists" (p. 65).

There is, it is true, plenty to say in favor of the *Cogito*, which antedates Descartes by centuries. Originating with Saint Augustine, it remains one of the necessary, or at least possible, pillars of metaphysics. The only question is whether from that starting point one can arrive at realism. One could easily show, we believe, that Saint Augustine, logically or not, never required of thought that it should guarantee the existence of matter, and if one asks who first expected thought to perform such a task one comes back once again to Descartes. Now it is perfectly true that the *Cogito* allows me to reach being, and even, in a sense, an absolute being, since it is not because I think that I am but because I am that I think. However, the heart of the problem remains untouched: namely, if the being I grasp is only through and in my thought, how by this means shall I ever succeed in grasping a being which is anything other than that of thought?

Descartes believed it was possible, but even apart from a direct critique of the proof he attempted to give, history is there to show us that his attempt ends in failure. He who begins with Descartes cannot avoid ending up with Berkeley or with Kant. There is an inner necessity of metaphysical essences, and the progress of philosophy consists precisely in reaching an ever clearer understanding of the contents of these essences. That is just what happened in the case of

Descartes and the Cartesians. The real distinction between body and soul as posed by the *Sixth Meditation* left open the insoluble problem of the "communication of substances", and we shall find ourselves in the same blind alley if we return to its entrance. So to get back to realism, it won't do to stop at the man who took the first step on the road to idealism because we shall then be forced to go the whole of the rest of the road with his successors. The Cartesian experiment was an admirable metaphysical enterprise bearing the stamp of sheer genius. We owe it a great deal, even if it is only for having brilliantly proved that every undertaking of this kind is condemned in advance to fail. However, it is the extreme of naïvety to begin it all over again in the hope of obtaining the opposite results to those which it has always given, because it is of its nature to give them.

If, then, neo-scholasticism gives up the delusive method of the bridge, what becomes of its realism? L. Noël, with his usual penetration and with the continuity of thought worthy of a true philosopher, has reached the conclusion that to be at once scholastic and critical of any realism has to be an *immediate realism*. Indeed, "immediatism" becomes an absolute necessity once one claims one can grasp the object without using some sort of intermediary to reach it. He justifies his thesis mainly by an appeal to Thomistic principles of the most authentic kind, and principally to this: the object of the understanding is not the material thing in its concrete individuality, but its nonmaterial quiddity which, as such, can form a real unity with the intellect. Therefore, for good reasons, L. Noël considers the source of the misunderstandings that have multiplied around this question to lie in the tendency of the imagination to represent concepts and ideas as material things. We must, he tells us, give up the illusory idea of an outside and an inside; we must place ourselves in the order of intelligibility at the indivisible point where things and the mind meet, and we can then, without sacrificing anything to either, study their relationships (*Notes d'épistémologie thomiste*, p. 80).

We agree, and in doing so, realize that what we are conceding is no unimportant detail. L. Noël has touched the core of the question; and in our opinion he is not only right about it, but completely right. What we persist in asking ourselves, after following him this far, is in what sense it remains legitimate to consider such an attitude "a Thomistic and realist theory of knowledge". Thomistic without any doubt—but in what sense realist?

For someone whose mind has been formed or, if you prefer it, warped by years of historical studies, there is, in the first place, an external consideration which cannot fail to make him stop and think. Realism may possibly be a neo-scholastic doctrine. But it is definitely not a scholastic one. Neither Saint Thomas, nor Saint Bonaventure, nor Duns Scotus knew that term in the sense we use it today. The realists of the Middle Ages opposed the nominalists on a ground noticeably different from that which the problem of knowledge occupies today. The nominalists themselves, Ockham for example, opted for a sensualist empiricism of the crassest kind; by comparison with it the teaching of Saint Thomas looks more like idealism than anything else. The fact is, we are concerned with a different problem. The Middle Ages were long preoccupied with the nature of the concept, or of the notion which the intellect abstracts from the object; but they never doubted that its content was borrowed from the content of the object, still less that the object really existed.

The least one can say, if one admits the correctness of this remark, is that a scholastic realist could only have been a realist without knowing it, which is not perhaps impossible, but which sets the problem in terms requiring us to be more than usually watchful, since we are giving a name

to a doctrine quite different from the one it was originally
applied to. As used today, the word realism means in the
first place the opposite to idealism when it claims that it is
possible to pass from the subject to the object. Applied to
medieval metaphysics it means a doctrine in which the real
existence of the object is taken for granted, either because
one denies there is a problem to be solved here, or because
one is as yet unaware of such a problem.

Neo-scholastic realism would seem then to be in a very
ambiguous position, since it is committed to finding in a
particular doctrine the solution to a problem which that doctrine had no suspicion existed. One therefore understands at
one and the same time both the fundamental logic of L.
Noël's position and the difficulties inherent in it. In a sense,
and at first sight, it seems to offer nothing but advantages.
To say that realism in order to be Thomist must be "immediate" is to kill two birds with one stone, since by so doing
one avoids the contradictions which are inseparable from the
notion of a mediate realism, and one is able in some degree
to explain why Saint Thomas had no need to be aware of his
realism. But do not the very difficulties we hoped to overcome by eliminating mediate realism turn up again, after a
change of position, in immediate realism? I believe they do,
and that is what I would like to try and show.

If the word realism has any meaning at all, it signifies,
according to the definition given in A. Lalande's *Vocabulaire*:
"The doctrine which holds that being is independent of any
actual knowledge which knowing subjects can have of it; *esse*
is not equivalent to *percipi*, even when that word is used in
the widest sense." Can one then conceive of such a thing as
an immediate realism, that is to say, of a *percipi* containing an
esse with an independent existence of its own? Can thought
be asked to give, immediately or mediately, anything else
but thought? L. Noël believes it can, and—with a perfectly

correct understanding of what is required for the enterprise to succeed, were that possible—he seeks a point where things and the mind meet in an indivisible unity so that it can be the basis for that realist epistemology which modern thought demands and scholasticism has not bequeathed to us.

But this point, if it exists, is still thought, first and foremost. Consequently, whether one likes it or not, every epistemology, even an immediatist one, will start from a datum of thought where, by an effort of interior discrimination, it will try to grasp the object. Nevertheless, how can one take the view that this situation is entirely different from that of the *Cogito ergo sum*? Evidently, it is because I am that I think, but it is not in the least evident that it is because things exist that I think of them; the absolute being that the *Cogito* immediately delivers to me can only be my own and no other. In consequence, whether the operation by which I apprehend the object as distinct from myself be a process of induction and therefore mediate, or an immediate grasp, the problem remains the same. If one's starting point is a *percipi*, the only *esse* one will ever reach will be that of the *percipi*.

It is not surprising, therefore, that those who choose this path sooner or later come up against serious difficulties. Like its predecessors, immediate realism ends up with the curious paradox of trying to derive a realist metaphysics from the method of Descartes, the mother of all idealism. "All of epistemology is there", according to L. Noël, including the point of departure for metaphysics, and the fate of realism depends on this question: "Can we, or can we not arrive at things if we make our standpoint that of the *Cogito*?" (p. 38). No, we cannot, and if the fate of realism depends on this question, its fate is settled; it is impossible to extract from any kind of *Cogito* whatsoever a justification for the realism of Saint Thomas Aquinas.

Should one be astonished at these sinuous procedures and the difficulties they involve us in? Not in the least, if, as I believe, the problem of finding a critical realism is self-contradictory, like the notion of squaring a circle. To start with there was scholasticism; unquestionably, scholasticism believed in the existence of an object distinct from the subject—no one is in any doubt about that; but whenever scholasticism affirms this, it is as a postulate rather than as a conclusion. Later, idealism made its appearance: having decided to define reality in terms of thought, it first tried by this method to rejoin a reality independent of thought then abandoned the attempt. Only then did there come on the scene a realism which, determined to undo the work of idealism, did not realize that it itself only existed through, and thanks to, its adversary, that it was consequently one with it, and that in borrowing from it its very method of presenting the problem, had committed itself in advance, sooner or later, to giving its adversary the victory. The illusion, which people who make attempts of this kind suffer from, even when they struggle hardest against it, is that one can extract an ontology from an epistemology, and, by this or that method, discover in thought anything apart from thought. A something outside thought cannot be thought of. There could be no better formula to describe idealism. And by it idealism stands condemned, because philosophy can no more do without what is not thought (or things) than it can do without thought itself, and if one cannot get outside oneself to arrive at things when one makes thought the starting point, that proves that thought is not the point one should have started from.

It seems that one is led thereby into an impossible situation. It is obvious that scholasticism is not idealism. But if it is neither a mediate nor an immediate realism, what is it? Here we are, condemned to fall back into naïve realism—the charge so often made against scholasticism.

However, maybe there is a way out. But we must look for it in the right place.

That modern scholasticism is a realist philosophy is beyond question; there is no middle ground between idealism and realism. But it is not—so I believe—a naïve realism because it clearly recognizes the existence of idealism, the nature of the problem idealism poses, and the real or apparent force of its arguments. Modern scholasticism is a conscious realism, the fruit of reflection and considered choice, but which refuses to take as its foundation the solution of the problem set by idealism because the problem is posed in terms which, of necessity, imply idealism itself as a solution. In other words, surprising as the thesis may appear at first, scholastic realism is not a function of the problem of knowledge—very much the contrary would be true—but in it the real is posited as distinct from thought, the *esse* as distinct from the *percipi*, in virtue of a certain idea of what philosophy is, an idea which is the condition for the very possibility of philosophy. Scholastic realism is a methodical realism.

To give back scholastic realism its true meaning, we must first of all return to the philosophic attitude of the medieval thinkers and reject that of the idealists. At bottom this is what Kant himself did. No more than Saint Thomas Aquinas did he think it necessary to dispute the real existence of a noumenon distinct in itself from its appearance in us. Critical idealism is distinguished from the idealism of Berkeley by an underlying realism which altogether escapes criticism itself, but which also depends on a particular conception of what philosophy is and of the conditions necessary for its very possibility.

When any form of scholasticism lays claim to being a philosophy, it uses the word (making the necessary reservations required by its subordination to theology) with its classic meaning. Scholasticism is a philosophy (i.e., a study

of wisdom) that by definition is the science of first principles and of first causes. The truth of its conclusions, whatever they should be, will make itself apparent chiefly through
the evidence of those principles, and also through their sim-
plicity and fruitfulness. Its task, therefore, will be to find a
set of self-evident first principles which are in accord with
each other and with experience. If idealism had succeeded
in producing such a set of principles and proving their explan-
atory fruitfulness, scholasticism would have nothing to object
to. Unfortunately, exactly the opposite has happened, and
that is why Thomistic realism, although not founded on a
critique of knowledge, is not reduced to being a form of
naïve realism. It bases itself on the evidence of its principles, and justifies itself by a critique of idealism which shows
the impotence of that system of thought to build a viable
philosophy. This is not the place to develop that critique.
But I would like at least to say something about the two
principles which should motivate it.

First of all, every idealist philosophy of the Cartesian type,
because at the outset it identifies the philosophic method
with that of a particular science, necessarily ends by emptying philosophy of any content of its own and condemns
itself to being a scientism. It is not by chance that, prior
even to Comte and Littré, idealism ended there, because
whenever one uses a scientific method as one's philosophic
method, either the results obtained will be true and in that
case scientific, or they won't be scientific and won't be true.
If the chosen method is that of mathematics, as was the
case with Descartes, metaphysics remains provisionally possible because in both cases an a priori knowledge is on hand.
But if the method chosen for pattern is that of physics, as
was the case with Kant, metaphysics as a distinct form of
knowledge becomes impossible, because the reason has been
isolated from the understanding and deprived in advance of

the sense knowledge necessary to make it productive. Descartes, Kant, Comte all witness to the powerlessness of idealism to pass from criticism to positive construction. That they intended to save philosophy as a distinct science is not in doubt, and yet each of them was followed by a school of thinkers who refuted their *pars construens* in the name of their *pars destruens*. For the Cartesians of the eighteenth century, Descartes' metaphysics stood condemned by his method. For many of Kant's successors the *Critique of Pure Reason* proves in advance the futility of the *Critique of Practical Reason*. As for the successors of Comte, like Littré, they repudiate subjective positivism in the name of absolute positivism and regard philosophy as having no content apart from that of science. Like those mythical animals, the Catoblepas, all idealist philosophies devour their own feet without realizing it.

In the second place, a reflection on the results gained by history would show, I believe, that the reason the idealist method is the suicide of philosophy is because it engages philosophy in an inextricable series of internal contradictions that ultimately draw it into skepticism—which could be called self-liberation through suicide. Why should metaphysics go on reasserting its own existence if it can reach no positive conclusions, and how can it reach any positive conclusion by following the idealist method? Descartes at first believed that his method would save the positive achievements of scholasticism, but he had not realized that these results were part and parcel with the method that had obtained them. As a result of his influence, and that of the conclusions he established, reality was ceaselessly fragmented into imaginary entities which are so much false coin. In becoming what it is for abstract thought, everything splits into a couple of antinomical terms which the ingenuity of philosophers will never succeed in reuniting. That is why modern philosophy, insofar as it does not abdicate in favor of science, presents the appearance of a field of battle where irreconcilable shadows are locked in a struggle without end— thought against extension, subject against object, the individual against society—so many fragments of the real broken away from it by the analytical solvent of thought, which that same thought vainly tries to reintegrate.

What we must do first of all, therefore, is free ourselves from the obsession with epistemology as the necessary precondition for philosophy. The philosopher as such has only one duty: to put himself in accord with himself and other things. He has no reason whatever to assume a priori that his thought is the condition of being, and, consequently, he has no a priori obligation to make what he has to say about being depend on what he knows about his own thought.

Without question one could maintain that the opposite is true, and one could justly support that position. The philosopher as such has no grounds for thinking that his thought might not be the condition of being, and he can, if he wants to, assume the task of reconstructing the universe by taking thought as his starting point. A priori the procedure is so plainly lawful that not only did Descartes try it, but no one up to now has found any valid objection to the *Cogito*, as such. *I think therefore I am* is a truth, but it is not a starting point. What justifies the opposite method is the fact that the *Cogito* is manifestly disastrous as a foundation for philosophy when one considers its terminal point. With a sure instinct as to what was the right way, the Greeks firmly entered on the realist path and the scholastics stayed on it because it led somewhere. Descartes tried the other path, and when he set out on it there was no obvious reason not to do so. But we realize today that it leads nowhere, and that is why it is our duty to abandon it.

So there was nothing naïve about scholastic realism; it was the realism of the traveler with a destination in view who, seeing that he is approaching it, feels confident he is on the right road. And the realism we are proposing will be even less naïve since it is based on the same evidence as the old realism and is further justified by the study of three centuries of idealism and the balance sheet of their results. The only alternatives I can see today are either renouncing metaphysics altogether or returning to a pre-critical realism. This does not at all mean that we have to do without a theory of knowledge. What is necessary is that epistemology, instead of being the pre-condition for ontology, should grow in it and with it, being at the same time a means and an object of explanation, helping to uphold, and itself upheld by, ontology, as the parts of any true philosophy mutually will sustain each other. I remember hearing Professor A. N. Whitehead give his students at Harvard this piece of advice, which seems to me very profound: "When you find your theory of knowledge won't work, it's because there is something wrong with your metaphysics." To this I would add, for my part, a further remark: in idealism nothing works. One ought not therefore to look for the remedy to idealism along the idealist path. The only conceivable remedy is to change one's metaphysics. No one can overcome idealism by opposing it from inside, because one cannot oppose it in such a way without surrendering to it. Idealism can only be overcome by dispensing with its very existence.

II

Realism and Method

Methodical Realism is simply an attempt to present the problem of Thomistic realism and suggest a slightly different interpretation from the sometimes accepted ones. However, this presentation of the question raises several other questions. In particular, it assumes that the solutions set aside by it have been sufficiently examined, correctly understood, and fairly criticized. So the essential points will have to be taken up one by one and an attempt made to justify them.

This is what I am going to try and do, first of all eliminating the objections brought against the solutions I propose and leaving until later the business of confirming them. The two stages of the inquiry are in fact independent of each other. Assuredly, if one of the theories I discuss were true it would be absolutely useless to look for another; but the converse is not necessarily so, because even if all the preceding theories were false it would not mean that mine was true; there would only perhaps be one more false theory, and there are enough of those already.

The most reasonable order to follow, therefore, seems to be this: first to define the positions already adopted, which I shall attempt to do by discussing two forms of neo-scholastic realism, mediate realism and immediate realism; then discuss the merit of those positions; and finally, insofar as they would seem to be not entirely satisfactory, try to define and justify a third.

To be as exact as possible, the problem I am going to discuss is the problem of metaphysical realism, properly so-called, and not the problem of the critique of knowledge. Critical philosophy is simply one of the various forms of idealism, even if a form which, in certain cases, can distinguish itself from idealism to the point of disowning idealism. The precise problem we have to deal with, therefore, is that of knowing why certain neo-scholastics maintain that the outside world exists. It is their reasons for affirming this, and their ways of affirming it, and only that, which I am going to explain, first as they appear in the teaching of Cardinal Mercier, and then in that of the most authoritative of his interpreters.

Mediate Realism and the Principle of Causality

The problem of the existence of the outside world has a place in Cardinal Mercier's system only as one of the necessary steps in proving the objective reality of abstract concepts. To establish that the content of our concepts is something other than a purely mental reality, a simple appearance or image without objective significance, one must first establish that "the object of our intelligible forms is materially contained in the sensible forms it is attributed to by our judgment", and then it must be proved that "the object of the sensible forms is real." [1]

We will grant the first of these two points without discussion. If there is an exterior world, and if that exterior

[1] All the quotations by Mercier in this chapter are taken from his *Critériologie générale ou théorie générale de la certitude*, 7th ed. (Louvain-Paris, 1918). See particularly p. 352 and pp. 358–60.

world is knowable by concepts, we could never form those concepts unless our minds communicated with that exterior world by means of a sensory grasp. One can deny, as Malebranche did, that any communication of this kind is possible, but then one will have to conclude with him that the external world, if it exists, is not the object of our conceptual thinking. However, it is a reality *outside the mind* which the criteriology we are considering wants to grasp. Thus this criteriology has good reasons for seeking the material of our concepts—*non causa, sed materia causae* [not the cause, but the material of the cause]—in the data of sense.

One can also easily see why the second point is necessary. All we have admitted by the first is the existence of a sense datum in the mind without knowing yet whether that datum corresponds to a real object outside the mind. The second proposition is so far from being necessarily linked with the first that Berkeley would never allow that the second could be deduced from it.

The problem, therefore, as it is here presented, is as follows: Is there any means of establishing with certainty that a non-mental reality exists? If not, we are forced to deny that our concepts have any truly objective reality, in the sense which a realist philosopher gives to that word. If the answer is yes, there is nothing to hinder us from admitting that the reality whose existence is thus proved is precisely the reality our intellect communicates with through our senses. One would indeed necessarily have to admit it, if the existence of that reality were to be posited as the sole conceivable cause of the content of our concepts. And that is precisely the course which this criteriology invites us to follow. How can it be shown that "there is something real corresponding to our sensory forms, a thing in itself"?

To prove this point, neo-scholastic realism has at its disposal two data: a fact of experience to be interpreted, and a principle to be applied to that fact so that with its support it can pass beyond it. The principle does not raise any difficulty, not at least for anyone who takes it up at the stage this criteriology has reached. The principle in question is that of causality, whose objective value has been previously established by philosophical analysis. As for the fact of experience, its nature is more difficult to grasp, and here we must pause a moment.

What we are dealing with is the sense of an inner experience, and this experience, taken in itself, is essentially *internal*. No one, not even the most determined phenomenalists such as John Stuart Mill for example, can or does deny that in all external perception our consciousness gives us as a twofold fact the existence of the perceiving subject and that of the object perceived. The question here is not of determining whether this feeling is well founded or whether it is an illusion. What matters is the fact itself, whose existence is undeniable. Rightly or wrongly, we have an inner and direct conviction that the exterior world exists. This is the starting point for the proof, but it is only the starting point because it remains to be proved—and this is the whole issue—that the exterior world in fact does exist. To achieve this, let us first analyze the inner experience, which has so far only been defined.

What it essentially involves is an impression of passivity. "Consciousness tells us that we are passive in regard to our sensations. When, while walking in the fields, I contemplate the blueness of the sky, hear the singing of the birds, smell the scents in the air, feel the ground under my feet, I sense that things are taking place inside me which do not come from me; I *submit to impressions* of light, song, scents, touch, resistance." This is the first point.

The second point establishes the contingency of these impressions. Since they are born, last for a time, and disappear to be reborn once more, it follows that their existence is not in itself necessary. It equally follows that their existence depends on something other than themselves—on something which causes them to be born and to exist; stops producing them and they disappear; produces them again and they reappear. In a word, their manifest contingency obliges us to look for a cause. This is why the principle of causality will be applied to the content of our sensations—to provide a sufficient reason for them.

At this point in the analysis, two hypotheses and only two remain possible; either I am the cause of my sensations, or something other than myself is. We know, from having established their contingency, that they are not their own cause. Their cause, therefore, can only be myself or something which is neither I nor they. But I cannot be their cause, for "I do not create the impressions myself, since on the contrary I *submit* to them." There must therefore be outside me a reality, a substance, independent of my thought, having an existence distinct from mine and which, as active cause, produces the events of which my sense impressions are only the passive result. From this we are led to the following conclusion: "Sensations presuppose something independent of my mental representations, a being or beings capable of making us experience sense impressions"—which is what had to be proved.[2]

There can be no question that the conclusion of such a criteriology is a realist one, but what kind of realism are we talking about? In the first place, a mediate realism; that seems

---

[2] Cardinal Mercier refers his readers in a note to two studies which he considers specially worthy of attention: G. Uphues, *Das Bewusstsein der Transzendenz* (Leipzig: O. R. Reisland, 1904), and *Ueber die Existenz der Aussenwelt*, a separately printed article from *Neue pädagogische Zeitung*, no. 31, 1894. I regret that I do not know either of these studies, because one might find in them a way out of the difficulties which seem inherent in his position.

clear. To begin with an internally experienced feeling, and then to infer the external reality of its object by means of the principle of causality, is manifestly to introduce between the psychological experience and its object an intermediary, which is itself the proof. This has nevertheless been denied, and the denial comes from a philosopher with such an intimate knowledge of Cardinal Mercier's thought that one cannot pass it by without examining its value.[3]

According to Monsignor Noël—and I shall have to come back to the point when discussing him in his own right—there is no need to bring in the principle of causality in order to establish the existence of external reality. In his eyes "the existence of anything real is given directly to consciousness. When I know something real, what is immediately given to my consciousness is the real object. To reach it no steps are necessary; only a full awareness of what one knows." In a position of this kind, thinks Monsignor Noël, there is no resort to *illationism*, and he can be taken at his word without danger of incurring any liabilities since he is talking about his own system. But he goes further, and one cannot suppress a feeling of surprise when he maintains that Cardinal Mercier has never subscribed to *illationism*. He bases his case on the argument that the "sense of an inner experience" which provides the grounds for affirming the exterior world's existence, implies, by its very passivity, belief in the reality of the sensory world as something not simply part of myself, with a reality apart from mine, and which is consequently not a simple psychological phenomenon.[4] No

[3] The question has already been raised by L. Rohellec, in *Revue thomiste* (1913, 21st year): 459–60. See Monsignor Noël's reply, same journal (1914, 22nd year): 205–12.

[4] L. Noël, *Notes d'épistémologie thomiste* (Louvain-Paris, 1925), pp. 220–22. I am indebted to my friend M. l'abbé G. B. Phelan, director of the Institute of Medieval Studies, Toronto, for throwing much light on the exact meaning of

doubt the experience implies this, but is that enough to justify considering such a realism an immediate realism?

One has only to consult Cardinal Mercier himself to recognize that it is nothing of the sort. If his proof has any kind of meaning, if indeed it even is a proof, it is precisely because our inner feeling about the reality of the external world does not by itself amount to a proof of its existence. It is the necessary starting point, but it is no more than that. And what does this starting point give us? "In our acts we directly perceive an *internal* reality" (the italics are the Cardinal's). In other words, we start with the immediate perception that consciousness believes in a real existence, but this fact of our internal experience does not authorize the intellect to affirm ipso facto the existence of the reality that corresponds to it. "We have a *direct* sense intuition of outside things, and, without intermediaries, we form for ourselves the *abstract idea* of what they are." And, in fact, since our sensory intuition involves the spontaneous positing of a universe outside the mind, it is certainly a sensory intuition of outside things, in the sense that the things it grasps are immediately presented to it as being outside. But an immediate sensory intuition of outside things is in no way equivalent to an intellectual certitude of the reality of their existence.

What our sense perceptions deliver to us is and always will be the phenomenon of knowledge itself in which, in fact, the sensory in act and the sensing subject in act are identical. What the abstract notion of the object delivers us is and always will be that phenomenon of consciousness in which the intelligible in act and the intellect in act are

---

the teaching in this book. I hope he will allow me to express my gratitude, while adding that he should not be held responsible for any errors my interpretation may contain, still less for the reservations I may have to express about Monsignor Noël's method, since he certainly would not agree with either.

identical. If this immediate ontological realism were not given, the internal feeling which expresses it would not exist, and criteriology would have nothing left to support it in order to prove the existence of the outside world. But conversely, if this ontological realism were at the same time a criteriological realism (in which case it would be an immediate criteriological realism), one no longer sees why it would still be necessary to demonstrate the exterior world's existence, since it would be given directly, not only in itself, but even for the intellect.

What on the contrary characterizes Cardinal Mercier's position is that the proof of the exterior world's existence is required by it (mediate criteriological realism) in order that the intellect, going beyond the raw fact of inner experience, may affirm with certainty that the outside world exists and that it is grasped directly by the senses (immediate ontological realism). The reasoning by which the intellect establishes the reality of its object as outside the mind may remain unperceived: "In the ordinary course of life we shall not recognize this appeal to a principle other than that of direct intuition, so familiar are we with its use. Habit diminishes the effort of attention and, as a result, the consciousness of what we are doing." Nevertheless, this activity goes on, and since "direct intuition" is not enough, reasoning must supplement it. It must be so, because if intuition is insufficient it is not because it is not direct, but because it is only sense intuition and therefore, though valid, incapable of guaranteeing by itself alone its own validity. So one must choose. "A number of thinkers refuse to admit that one must have recourse to the principle of causality in order to assure oneself that the outside world exists. They happily persuade themselves that we have a direct intuition of its existence. We are convinced they are mistaken."

There we have Cardinal Mercier's position, put as strongly as possible, and it is the Cardinal himself who states it.

And here is Monsignor Noël's position, as he describes it: "I have said that, in my opinion, the principle of causality should not be introduced in order to establish the existence of reality."

From which it follows that one of two things must be true. Either the reality whose existence Monsignor Noël reaches directly is not external, in which case the proof of that external existence has still to be produced and his realism will not be immediate, or this reality is an external reality, in which case it makes Cardinal Mercier's proof completely useless. I don't see anything to bother about in that, the contrary rather, since I regard the proof as useless too. But I want to understand exactly what Monsignor Noël's position is, because if he is really in agreement with Cardinal Mercier, I have to admit that I do not in the least understand what he is saying, or I no longer understand what immediate realism means. One of them says: I can't do without the principle of causality. The other says: I have no need of it. Up to this point I understand what they are saying. But if one of the two adds that he is in agreement with the other, and this is really so, I do not see what possible meaning can be given to any one of the three foregoing propositions.

Let us suppose it granted that Cardinal Mercier's realism is not a direct realism. It will then be possible to compare it with other mediate realisms, particularly Descartes', and thereby see to what extent this neo-scholasticism is faithful to the tradition it claims to belong to, or is on the contrary moving away from it.

To demonstrate the existence of the exterior world, what does Descartes demand? First and foremost, sensation.[5] Ideas

---

[5] For a detailed analysis of this question, see *Études sur le rôle de la pensée médiévale dans le système cartésien* (Paris: J. Vrin, 1930), pp. 234–44. I ought to add that my interpretation of Descartes' proof is neither the classical one nor beyond criticism. The received interpretation would have it that Descartes

would not provide a firm enough platform to support the process of induction he is going to embark on. Because intelligible by themselves, our ideas need no efficient cause other than the intellect which forms them. The clear and distinct idea of extension, for instance, considered in its pure intelligibility, could be conceived by an intellect even if such a thing as real extension did not exist. One could add, moreover, that the same goes for the image of extension. Without doubt this is a more delicate matter because, as it unquestionably seems to me, in the effort of imagining it, our intellect turns to the body with which it is united and, so to speak, attaches itself to that. The probability that such a body, and the bodies acting on it, really exist becomes from then on very great. Nevertheless, it is still no more

---

proves the exterior world essentially by invoking God's truthfulness, which guarantees our natural belief in its existence. Monsignor Noël seems to adopt an interpretation of this kind. In his view, the Cartesian proof does not depend on the principle of causality (L. Noël, *Réalisme méthodique ou réalisme critique?* Académie Royale de Belgique, Classe des Lettres et des Sciences morales et politiques, 5e série, t. XVII, pp. 111–29; see particularly p. 124: "Descartes believed ..." and p. 129: "It is true, Descartes ..."), and he would perhaps deny at one and the same time that either Descartes' or Cardinal Mercier's proof rests on this principle. As far as Descartes is concerned, I believe that the object of appealing to the natural belief in the outside world's existence is to eliminate God as a possible cause of our ideas, but nothing more than that. This belief we have, even guaranteed by a truthful God, would not be a proof, because it is not a clear and distinct idea; at least it only becomes that when it makes itself explicit by an analysis of the passivity of sensation and a reasoned application of the principle of causality. If my interpretation of Descartes is incorrect, there will be no Cartesianism in Cardinal Mercier's thought, even of an unconscious kind. If it is correct, that does not prove that my interpretation of Cardinal Mercier is, or vice versa. Finally, I add that the purpose of the present work is not to reply to Monsignor Noël's penetrating observations. I hope to come back to them when examining the critical problem because it seems to me it was at this point above all that his article was aimed. I do not even believe we use the word "critical" in the same sense, nor, consequently, that we are as far from each other as we might seem.

than a probability, for after all this image of extension is still clear and distinct, it belongs therefore to the intelligible order, and it is without question my mind which forms it. My mind can even form it at will, and the activity it deploys in forming it seems to indicate that it is dependent on my mind, and on nothing else.

Sensation is quite another matter. It differs from idea and image, first in that it always carries with it that inner and irresistible feeling that what it presents is something really existing, not only in us, but in itself and independently of us. This feeling is so powerful, that it is what lies at the source of Aristotelian philosophy and scholasticism. Secondary qualities would not be taken as real in these systems if it were not the spontaneous reaction of the human mind to affirm that they are real. We are dealing with precisely the same kind of feeling required by Cardinal Mercier. "Indeed, considering the ideas of all these qualities which presented themselves to my thought and which alone I truly and directly felt, it was not without reason I believed I was experiencing things quite distinct from my thoughts, in other words bodies from which these ideas proceeded."[6] Here we have the first step in the proof: a sensory intuition that posits the reality of its object.

And now the second step. What Cardinal Mercier's analysis discloses is the passive and involuntary character of sensation, a something, consequently, suffered or undergone. Let us simply continue reading what Descartes has to say about these sensory ideas. "It was brought home to me that they appeared to it (my thought) without my consent being required, so that I could not sense any object, however much I wanted to, if it was not present to one of my organs of sense; and that if it was so present, it was in no way possible

---

[6] R. Descartes, *Méditations métaphysiques*, VIe médit., ed. Adam-Tannéry, t. IX, p. 59. The text which follows can be found in the same place.

not to sense it." The problem then becomes that of knowing how, apart from this interior feeling, that things do exist, and from these passive sensations it is going to be possible to establish the reality of their object.

In both cases, it goes without saying, appeal will be made to the principle of causality. We have seen that this is the way chosen by Cardinal Mercier, and Descartes followed the same path before him. The philosopher's declarations are explicit. His statements were made in connection with the very problem before us.

> It is also a first principle that all reality and all perfection, which is only objectively in our ideas, must be formally and eminently in their causes; and all the opinions we have ever had about the existence of things outside our minds rest solely on that. For where could the notion that they exist have come from, if not exclusively from the belief that they have reached our minds from the senses.[7]

My readers will I hope forgive me for insisting on the point, but Descartes' position has been misunderstood so often that it is necessary to clarify it as much as possible, and the simplest way of doing that is to quote his own words.[8] He is concerned with what are for him fundamental and self-evident axioms.

> I. There is nothing that exists of which one cannot ask why it exists. IV. All the reality and perfection in

[7] R. Descartes, *Secondes réponses*, vol. 9, p. 107.

[8] The text which follows is taken from "Axioms or general notions in the Reasons which prove God's existence and the distinction which exists between the human mind and body presented geometrically", in ibid., pp. 127–28.

a thing is to be found formally, or eminently, in its first and total cause. V. From which it follows that the objective reality of our ideas requires a cause ... And it should be noticed that this axiom is so necessary and undeniable that the knowledge of everything, sensible as well as insensible, depends on it. How, for instance, do we know that the sky exists? Is it because we see it? But this seeing only touches the mind insofar as it is an idea; an idea, I say, inherent in the mind itself and not something pictured in the imagination. And when this idea occurs, we cannot conclude that the sky exists except by supposing that there must be a cause for the objective reality of every idea, a cause which itself really exists; which cause, we decide, must be the sky itself, and the same with everything else.

One only has to re-read the *Sixth Meditation* in the light of these passages in order to verify the fact that the entire proof of the real existence of extension rests on the principle of causality.

But let us resume our course.

If I have passively experienced sensations, then they must have a cause. I cannot be their cause, because if I suffer them I do not produce them.

Moreover, I find in myself a certain passive faculty for feeling (that is to say for receiving and knowing) ideas of sensory things. But it would be useless to me, and I could in no way employ it, if there were not in myself or in other beings a separate and active faculty capable of forming and producing these ideas. However this active faculty cannot be in myself insofar as I am only a thing which thinks, seeing that it does not presuppose my thought, and also that those ideas have often presented themselves to me without any contribution on my part, and often even against my will. They must therefore necessarily subsist in some substance other than mine. . . . And that substance is either a body, that is to say a corporeal nature . . . or it is God himself. . . . Now since God does not deceive, it is manifest He does not send me these ideas directly Himself. . . . For not having given me any faculty for recognizing that He does, but on the contrary a strong inclination to believe that they are sent to me or come from corporeal things, I do not see how one could exempt Him from acting deceitfully if in fact these ideas originated with or were produced by some other cause than corporeal things. Consequently one is compelled to admit that corporeal things exist.

What more could one want? Indeed he says almost too much, and it is that which may have misled people about the real nature of Descartes' thought.

There is a fairly widespread opinion that Descartes proves the existence of the exterior world by invoking God's truthfulness. That is not entirely correct. Descartes establishes the existence of bodies by proving that they are the only possible cause of our passive sensations. He only brings God into the business because, once our own thought has been eliminated, there still remain two possible exterior causes of sensation: God or bodies. God's truthfulness is introduced simply so that we can exclude God and keep bodies. Therefore he does not prove the existence of the exterior world by asking the divine truthfulness to guarantee our spontaneous belief in the reality of its existence, but by establishing its existence through a causal induction, and by showing that no cause of sensation is conceivable except corporal things and they alone.

I am not here trying to pretend that Cardinal Mercier was a disciple of Descartes, even if an unconscious one. On the contrary, his criteriology teems with lively criticisms of Cartesianism and its method. But one cannot deny that the steps by which his thought reaches the outside world is in some respects analogous to the Cartesian proof of the existence of bodies. In both cases, one and the same inner experience makes it possible to affirm the reality of its object by invoking one and the same first principle of knowledge, namely, the principle of causality. One could not maintain there is immediatism in Descartes without making oneself ridiculous, since his whole method consists in deducing the existence of an extension, genuinely distinct from thought, from a thought genuinely distinct from extension. In his system, the problem of making the transition is so real that his successors declared it to be impossible, all of which resulted in the occasionalism of Malebranche, the parallelism of Spinoza, the pre-established harmony of Leibniz, and the pure idealism of Berkeley. How, then, has it been possible to maintain, and can it still be maintained, that what cannot be said of Descartes can be said of Cardinal Mercier? If Descartes' proof excludes any kind of immediate realism, why is it thought possible to hold that Cardinal Mercier's implies it? That is the question we have to tackle next.

The Reduction to Immediatism

As we have seen, the attempt to reduce the proof to immediatism has been made by Monsignor Noël.

I have to admit that I cannot follow his conclusions and I have just said why. Between Cardinal Mercier, who asserts that, without the principle of causality, it is impossible to reach any kind of existence outside the mind, and Monsignor

Noël, who asserts that as soon as I have passive sensations, the intimately experienced feeling implies, in Cardinal Mercier's thought, the existence of a world of sensory things independent of myself, I feel myself compelled to stick by the actual text of the philosopher whose thought has to be interpreted. This, however, raises another problem.

Assuming there is illationism in the proof in question, why does Monsignor Noël say there isn't any? Monsignor Noël has a much better knowledge and a much more intimate understanding of the Cardinal's thought than I have. I realize that a school of thought is not just a group of men who repeat each other, but at the very least consists of a group of minds inspired by the same principles, which they live by and know from within, and who are consequently in a position to determine what those principles mean. I cannot, therefore, find myself disagreeing with Monsignor Noël over the interpretation of Cardinal Mercier's thought without feeling the need, and indeed the duty, to seek the really deep-seated reasons for the interpretation he gives. For unless I am completely mistaken, it is possible that I am more faithful to the letter, while he is more faithful to the spirit. The certainty that this was so would not be without importance for the interpretation of Monsignor Noël's own thought and for the final solution of the problem. I will try, therefore, to get at the meaning of and reasons for his interpretation.

The first point to consider is the fact that in this interpretation what the Cardinal calls *existence* is what should rather be called *reality*, or, if the word *existence* is to be kept, it does not refer to the actuality of the thing itself, but to a simple *non-self*. Let us consider an example of each of these two cases.

Recalling the analysis of the "sense of an inner experience" with which the proof starts, Monsignor Noël asks, "Can one believe that the author who writes this thinks of the whole ensemble of the sensible world as simply part of the self, as having no other reality, as being a purely psychological phenomenon?"[9] My reply is no. As with Descartes, this feeling immediately implies an irresistible belief in the existence of a world distinct from myself, existing in itself, and very different from a mere psychological phenomenon. In other words, there is no question of our having to surmount a spontaneous illusion that what seems to us real is not. And it is true that, for Cardinal Mercier, sensation immediately posits a non-self. But the reality thus posited is still only the "existence of an *inner reality*", and one which does not allow us "to *maintain with certainty the existence* of one or more realities *outside the mind* without bringing in the principle of causality" (italics in original). This leads me to ask myself the following questions. When interpreting Cardinal Mercier's text, what meaning does Monsignor Noël attribute to it? Does he mean that the sense of an experience by itself (and therefore before the use of the principle of causality) gives us the existence of a reality outside the mind? If the answer is yes, it flatly contradicts the text. Or does he mean that what the experience in question gives us is no more than a reality given as distinct from myself in and through my thought (prescinding from its existence)? If the answer is yes, it seems to me to agree perfectly with Cardinal Mercier, but then an inference will still be needed and the realism will no longer be immediate.[10]

---

[9] Noël, *Notes d'épistémologie thomiste*, p. 222.

[10] I find the same ambiguity on the following page (p. 223): "It is quite clear that he regards us as grasping immediately something other than psychical states of mind." Yes, that is clear enough. What is not clear is what this other something is. Is it simply the apprehension of a non-self by thought, or is it the certainty that what I think of as a non-self is an independent existence? What I am given is not a sensation (a psychical state taken as an object) but a tree. Only for Cardinal Mercier it does not follow that the tree exists.

Let us now take an example of the second case.

"Consequently," Monsignor Noël writes, "if Cardinal Mercier has recourse to the principle of causality, can we suppose he does this in order to establish the existence of a non-self?"[11] Certainly not. Sensation by itself gives us the existence of a non-self, but it is insufficient to convince us that this non-self, which—let us not forget this—is an "*internal* reality", also exists as an *extramental* reality. Let us continue with the same passage.

"This seems to me most unlikely. On the contrary, it appears to me certain that he considers the non-self a primary datum." I agree. But we are talking about a primary datum which is part of an "internal" experience and which gives us "immediately" only the "existence of an *internal* reality".[12] So we come back, as always, to the same question, namely, when Monsignor Noël talks about reality does he mean by it what Cardinal Mercier calls existence, or does he not rather make the whole weight of his own thought, and consequently of his interpretation, bear on the first stage of the proof alone in order to show that everything else is already virtually implied in it? If this were so, everything else, that is to say even Cardinal Mercier's proof, would become useless; but one would then understand how it is possible, for Monsignor Noël does not set himself up as the official interpreter of Cardinal Mercier's thought. What he gives us is his understanding of what he discovers in his books and his teaching, adding the reflections he finds himself drawn into making by following the line of that thought.[13] Let us, therefore, follow him, since he is a guide who knows where he is going.

---

[11] Ibid.

[12] Mercier, *Critériologie*, p. 360.

[13] Noël, *Notes d'épistémologie thomiste*, p. 220.

The fundamental difficulty of the interpretation proposed to us seems to me to be this. Admitting that Cardinal Mercier does not make use of the principle of causality to prove the existence of the external world, nevertheless, since he still does make use of the principle, for what purpose does he do so? Monsignor Noël's reply is that the principle is not used to establish the existence of the non-self, but that of things-in-themselves. The question then presenting itself is to know what we are to understand by this latter term, and above all the nature of the reality which the principle of causality is going to allow us to reach.

To arrive at an understanding, we must try to grasp what a phenomenon is and what is its relationship to the thing-in-itself, when the question is presented in this fashion. We are told that the principle of causality will lead us from the phenomenon to the thing-in-itself. Will the transition be from a thing to the same thing, or from a thing to some other thing? If the transition is to be purely and simply from a thing to the same thing, then the principle of identity will be sufficient, and we will have no need of the principle of causality. If the transition is to be from one thing to another, it will be impossible.

It would seem, therefore, that the phenomenon (that is to say, "the non-self given directly to consciousness") both is, and at the same time is not, the thing-in-itself. Conversely, one should perhaps say that the thing-in-itself in a certain sense is the phenomenon; it is the phenomenon insofar as it is given to consciousness, so much so that "between the thing and the phenomenon there is no radical opposition; the phenomenon is simply the aspect the thing takes on for us".[14]

One has to agree that if this really is the case then Cardinal Mercier's line of argument would not be an inference

[14] Ibid., p. 224. Cf. pp. 37–40.

or that, at any rate, such an inference would be from the existence of the thing known under one mode to the existence of the same thing known under another mode. This, it seems to me, explains why the disciples of Cardinal Mercier refuse to see any kind of illation in his proof, and if their interpretation is correct, they are absolutely right. The existence I am going to reach is already given to me from the very instant I am aware of it, and the only function of the principle of causality will be to enable me to reach it in a different and better fashion. All that has to be established is whether Cardinal Mercier's teaching supports the interpretation, or even allows room for it. Here let me insist that I am not at this stage disputing the intrinsic value of a position of this kind. I simply want to know whether this really is what Cardinal Mercier's teaching signifies, because one cannot discuss the value of a teaching before understanding what it means.

I see at least one difficulty in the foregoing interpretation. It forgets, or seems to me to forget, the distinction expressly mentioned by Cardinal Mercier himself, between the relationship of reality to the intellect in the phenomenon of knowing, and the relationship between the knowing self and the known non-self. If "the principle of identity is insufficient for posing the existence of a non-self" [15] is it not precisely because the *existence* of the non-self is something different from that of the self?

Now as soon as one thinks about it, one sees that this clearly is the reason. No doubt in the act of knowing, the actuality of subject and of object is one. But the existence which the intellect posits when it asserts the existence of the external world is something other than its own and of its representation. When I perceive and conceive an object,

[15] Mercier, *Critériologie*, p. 360.

there are two existences: the existence of the object and the existence of the knowing subject, which includes that of its mental images—and there are no others. The common actuality of subject and object leaves intact the purely analogical character of their subjective existences. They are not two distinct beings which become an *idem numero*, but only one being, that of the subject, which, thanks to its sense faculties, participates in the actuality of another being without the existence of the subject becoming the same as the object's, nor the object's that of the subject's. The proof is that the form of the object remains its form, and that if the knowledge of one by the other is their common act, this is because between the form of one and the other there is henceforth an identity—not a numerical identity but a formal one, *convenientia in forma*.

If this is really how things are, the possibility of deriving the proof of the external world's existence from immediate realism seems doubtful.

One can easily see that it is the existence of the thing itself which we know in the phenomenon. One can even more easily understand that there need be no radical opposition between the thing and the phenomenon, but on the contrary, that they perfectly fit each other. On the other hand, it is much more difficult to understand how the being of the phenomenon, which is simply that of the knowing subject, can at the same time be that of the object known, which is exclusively that of the thing.

A common act in the order of intentionality cannot transform itself into a common act in the order of existence; on the contrary, it presupposes two distinct existences. If, therefore, the real purpose of Cardinal Mercier's proof is, as I believe, to infer from the existence of something in thought the existence of something outside thought—"if, in the phenomenon of knowledge, the intelligible *in act* and the intellect *in act* are identical, it is quite otherwise with the knowing self and the known non-self"—how can we pass from the existence of the knowing self and its mental images to the known non-self, whose existence is not identical with our own, without resorting to an inference? Either this inference will be from the existence of the thing-in-itself known as a phenomenon to the existence of the thing-in-itself as itself, in which case one will have an immediate realism; but if we are talking about one and the same existence we shall really have proved nothing in regard to its existence, since we shall have already granted that.[16] Or the inference will be from a phenomenal being to another kind of being having a separate existence, in which case Cardinal Mercier's proof is an authentic proof, but his realism is no longer immediate. It is—though with a different spirit and a sense of its own—a realism whose procedure is analogous to Descartes', namely, a proof of the existence of things outside the mind which specifically cause the passive impressions we have of them.

Immediate Realism

It is time now to look at the position of immediate realism in terms of itself and independently of its actual or possible connections with Cardinal Mercier's thought.

The two problems are not necessarily related. Monsignor Noël could have made the thought of the School of Louvain's

[16] I am not saying that the inference would be philosophically valueless, since it would change our mode of knowing the object; but it would be valueless as far as the actual existence of the object is concerned, since it would be that same existence which would first be given as a phenomenon then as an in-itself. In reality, the existence of the phenomenon is part of my existence, since it is the activity of the thinking being which supports it. It, therefore, remains distinct from that of the object.

founder seem closer to his own than is quite legitimately possible—as I fear may be the case, though I am not quite sure about it—without having thereby endangered his own position. So it is in itself and on its own account that I must now examine it. In doing so, I shall try as much as possible to avoid repeating what I have already said. The only thing about it I want to recall is that the problem dividing us is not a problem of metaphysics but one of method. Monsignor Noël is a committed realist. So am I. But we are looking for the best way of formulating our realism and of conceiving its nature. Monsignor Noël identifies himself with the medieval tradition. So do I. But we are trying to discover, each in our own way, how its principles can be made to throw light on the problems of our time, and I am not sure that we understand that tradition in quite the same way. These are the only questions that are at issue, but they are real questions.

As soon as one accepts the idea of immediate realism, there can, by definition, no longer be any question of demonstrating or proving the existence of the outside world. One only has to find it, or, as Monsignor Noël says, show it. Therefore, the sole problem remains that of knowing how to show it, and it is precisely here that our methods differ. Since I have permitted myself some reservations about Monsignor Noël's method, I will try to justify them. But first of all, what is his method?

Essentially, it consists in starting from the immediate data of consciousness, accepted as such. Several advantages are said to flow from this "because it provides the majority of philosophers with a common ground", which at least allows them to agree about the initial data of the problem, and consequently, with these initial data as a basis, it will be possible to "start a conversation".

The immediate realist is not, therefore, someone who regards the existence of the outside world as doubtful; he is not even a person who, without doubting its existence, feels the need to prove it. He is simply someone who sees the real as directly given, but who is searching for the best way of making us see that for us as much as for him it is really something given. "I am well aware", he says, "that the real is among the immediate data of consciousness, but it is not the first thing I believe I have to show." [17] In other words, it is a question of using an intermediary to show an immediate datum; we have, consequently, to find a way of reaching it and to justify the usefulness of making such a detour.

Reality can be grasped at levels of different depths. It is immediately given to us in a kind of block form, which is simply the "apprehended reality". But nothing forbids us (we are told) from first considering within this block only one of its aspects, that is to say, "the apprehended". Further reflection shows us that "the apprehended" is something real, thus enlarging the notion of truth. And still further reflection will enlarge it very much more by showing that over and above human knowledge there exists another, and this time absolute knowledge, the divine knowledge. This procedure is simply a cutting up of "the theory of Saint Thomas who from the start places himself at the second stage. But why does he not think it necessary always to say so explicitly? And why does he not start from the third stage?" [18]

These are important questions indeed and I shall be coming back to them. For the time being, we should merely note the fact that this immediate realism, in order to start with the immediate data of consciousness, is planning, provisionally at least, to consider in the "apprehended" real only the "apprehended" without the reality.

[17] Noël, *Notes d'épistémologie thomiste*, p. 228.
[18] Ibid., pp. 228–29.

What can a formula of this kind possibly mean? I do not believe "the apprehended" is here meant to be understood as apprehension itself, otherwise we should have to pass, at least mentally from a simple "I feel" or "I think" to something in no way contained in them. What this expression signifies is rather the judgment, and in the case under discussion a judgment of existence independent of the reality whose existence it posits. Thus all one has shown is the "apprehended" as "apprehended" before showing it as real, and this time the transition will be lawful, since the "apprehended" is nothing but the real itself penetrating the mind in the form of knowledge. It explains, moreover—one sees it clearly at this point—why Monsignor Noël can read his own ideas into Cardinal Mercier's text without in any way violating the letter of it, because if the sense of an inner experience one starts with includes the existence of the real itself, the principle of causality will no longer be invoked at a later point to establish that existence. However that may be, Monsignor Noël's own thought is perfectly clear, and if his position is a subtle one, that is because the problem is. At no point can one say he is shut up inside consciousness, since, from the first moment, what his consciousness grasps is an apprehended something.

The only question one can still ask oneself, therefore, is whether the proposed method of showing reality is the most advantageous one, and first of all whether it makes the opening of discussion with non-scholastic philosophers easier. I cannot help feeling doubtful about it. If one adopts this procedure, everyone is going to think of Descartes, and Monsignor Noël himself invites us to do so by devoting a chapter to the *Cogito*. The trouble with this mode of proceeding is that it starts off the discussions on a misunderstanding, a serious enough matter if what one is hoping to derive from them is a practical advantage. As soon as an inquirer on the other side notices this misunderstanding, as he very rapidly will, we shall see him abandon the talks, convinced that the neo-scholastic, who only wanted to smooth the path to understanding, has not even grasped what the Cartesian approach to the question is.

Everyone in fact knows that with Descartes the *I think*, far from including a non-self present to thought, excludes by definition everything which is not strictly thought. It is indeed why in his system the principle of causality is necessarily required to reach the existence of a non-self separate from myself.

Here, on the contrary, the *Cogito* is charged from the outset with all the non-self it apprehends and which it explicitly grasps without the need of any subsequent illation. It here has the task, therefore, of introducing everything which in Descartes' system it was designed to exclude. Will realism make discussion easier by appearing to start as idealism, when it is really doing exactly the opposite? I doubt it. Besides, the immediate data of consciousness, as a reflective idealism conceives them, signify exactly the opposite of what they mean for realism, because the immediate data of the realist are the first of which Descartes—as before him Plato, and after him Bergson—rids himself in order to return by way of reflection to what for him is immediate, though last (for the realist). What is immediate to the idealist can be Ideas, Thought, Will, Duration, in a word no matter what, provided it is not the object. What point is there then in borrowing a language whose terms are in the truest sense equivocal? That is one question.

But there is another. One may perhaps get oneself listened to, but is one going to be understood? Is there not a risk, I mean, of creating misunderstanding about the very meaning of the truth one wants to have accepted? The epistemology proposed to us has already been criticized—quite unjustly in my view, insofar as it is accused of drawing Thomism in an idealist direction. One must have badly misread Monsignor Noël to make an objection of that kind; but the misjudgment would perhaps not have been made were it not for the fact that the method of explaining Thomism which he offers us is so little in keeping with the spirit of Thomism. The more anxious one is to keep it as it is, the more careful one must be not to try and pass it off as something other than it is. To treat what is apprehended as separate from reality, even if only as part of a methodological device, is to do the opposite of what Saint Thomas always did. And this brings us back to the questions put by Monsignor Noël. Why does Saint Thomas always start from reality and not from "the apprehended"? Why, too, does he not start from God?

The Thomistic Method

"The scholastics", said Spinoza, "start from things; Descartes from thought; I start from God."

He could not have said anything more true, and the name of Spinoza is enough to remind us why in fact the scholastics do not start from God.

Between the Christian God and things there is a metaphysical fissure, separating the necessary from the contingent. The world only exists by a free ordinance of God; consequently, it cannot be deduced from God. In fact, it is the opposite that is true—which shows how impossible the thing is. Not only can one not deduce the existence of the world from the existence of God, but equally, because we are ourselves part of the world, our knowledge comes up against the same metaphysical breach as our being. The human mind cannot have God as its natural and proper object. As a creature, it is directly proportioned only to created being, so much so that instead of being able to deduce the existence of things from God, it must, on the contrary, of necessity rest on things in order to ascend to God.

So the smallest trace of Spinozism would be enough to ruin Thomist epistemology.

No such radical break opposes Thomism to Cartesianism— far from it, for the two metaphysics are in agreement on more than one point. But their methods, at least, are irreducibly opposed. For Saint Thomas—and it is the very essence of realism—*ab esse ad nosse valet consequential* [from a thing's reality one can be certain of its possibility]. For Descartes— and it is the foundation stone of idealism—*a posse ad esse valet consequential* [from its possibility one cannot be certain of its reality]. Moreover, the opposition between these two methods rests on the opposition between two theories of knowledge. While Descartes finds being in thought, Saint Thomas finds thought in being. What is at issue is not a paradox, but what for Saint Thomas is an unshakeable truth. The thought in question is our thought. But our thought, left to its own resources, is strictly incapable of passing from the virtual knowledge it has of itself to an actual knowledge. On its own, it has the power of knowing, but not the power of knowing itself, because it only becomes capable of knowing itself in the act of knowing something else— that it may actually know it must have objects of sense, consequently things.[19] The actual situation of the intellect, as Saint Thomas sees it, is that if there were no things, there would be no knowledge, and this also explains why in his description of our perceptions he always starts by placing himself at the second stage. Indeed, as far as he is concerned, the first stage does not exist.

[19] Saint Thomas Aquinas, *Summa Theologiae*, I, 87, 1, resp.

When Saint Thomas tells us that the intellect reaches objects, things, no one can misunderstand what he means by that:

> Could we not say that the *res* Saint Thomas talks about, and which the judgment should conform to, although something objective and independent, is nevertheless in the mind? Anyone who thought that would be thoroughly wrong. If Saint Thomas does not feel it necessary to be explicit on the subject, it is probably because he never dreamed that anyone could misunderstand him. For him, the thing is plainly the real thing posited as an entity existing in its own right and outside human consciousness.[20]

Exactly so, and it could not be better put. But if this is the way things are, how can one maintain that in Thomism one can start from a something apprehended prescinding from its reality? Whatever object I apprehend, the first thing I apprehend is its being: *ens est quod primum cadit in intellectu* [being is what first strikes the intellect]. But this being which is the first object of the intellect—*ens est proprium objectum intellectus, et sic est proprium intelligibile* [being is the proper object of the intellect, and thus it is the specifically intelligible] [21]—is, in virtue of what has just been said, something entirely different from "an apprehended" without the reality; it is reality itself, given by means of an act of apprehension no doubt, but not at all as simply apprehended. In short, one could say that if the block which experience offers us for analysis needs to be dissected according to its natural articulations, it is still an "apprehended *reality*" which it delivers us, and unless we are going to alter the structure

[20] Noël, *Notes d'épistémologie thomiste*, p. 33.
[21] Aquinas, *Summa Theologiae*, I, 5, 2, resp.

of reality, no method authorizes us to present it merely as a "reality *apprehended*" (italics added).

Besides, one only has to reread the text of Saint Thomas to realize that the order he follows is not an accidental one, or something one can modify simply as a temporary expedient. The order lies at the heart of the teaching. For an intellect like ours, which is not its own essence, as God's would be, and whose own essence is not its natural object, as with the angels, that object must necessarily be something extrinsic. That is why the object which the intellect apprehends must be something extrinsic as such. The first thing it grasps is a nature inhabiting an existence which is not its own, the *ens* of a material nature. That is its proper object, *etideo id quod primo cognoscitur ab intellectu humano est hujusmodi objectum* [and therefore what the human intellect knows first is an object of this kind]. It is only secondarily that it knows the actual act by which it knows the object—*et secundario cognoscitur ipse actus, quo cognoscitur objectum* [and what is known secondarily is the act itself by which the object is known]. And finally it is by the act that the intellect itself is known—*et per actum cognoscitur ipse intellectus* [and through the act, the intellect itself is known].[22]

I am far from believing that Monsignor Noël confuses the second step with the first step, and still less that he wants to move the second into first place, but at the same time I doubt whether we have the right to divide the first in two, because what Saint Thomas says and psychological experience confirms is that what is first given us is the existence of things. And even supposing one should want to halve this experience, what ought to be shown first is not the apprehended thing but the existing thing. "The apprehended" is the extrinsic already inside the intrinsic, whereas

[22] Aquinas, *Summa Theologiae* I, 87, 3, resp.

the intellect tends directly, intentionally, toward the object as it is in itself and not as it is in us, that is to say, toward the extrinsic as extrinsic. Not to present scholastic realism according to its own understanding of itself is to try and get it accepted by a method not made for it.

In what then does it ultimately consist? The name one gives it matters little provided we are in agreement about what it means; and the method of exposition used has only a secondary importance too, if there is agreement about the fundamentals of the question. Scholastic realism does not rest on metaphysical reasoning. If that reasoning started from God it would inevitably miscarry, since it would come up against the impossibility of deducing the contingent from the necessary. If it started from thought, in the sense understood by Descartes, it would fail no less surely, although for a different reason. Between one kind of contingent being and another there is always a metaphysical gap due to the analogy of being. Again, if one starts with a being heterogeneous with respect to another one is trying to reach, one will never reach it because the being of the other will never be anything for the first but a likeness of its own manufacture.[23] So the only solution is to admit, as experience suggests, that rather than the subject finding its object through an analysis of knowledge, it discovers its knowledge, and itself, in the analysis of the object.

One is led by the above to make the existence of the outside world a matter of evidence, but the direct and concrete evidence of a sensory intuition, which translates itself

[23] It goes without saying that the impossibility of proving the existence of the outside world starting from thought of the Cartesian type in no way affects the proofs for the existence of God. Although one cannot deduce things from God, in starting with things one necessarily posits God because of their very contingency. And this time the principle of causality does play a part, precisely because the real on which it rests is already given to it. One moves from a perceived existence to a concluded existence, instead of, as idealism does, trying to infer an existence starting from a mental image.

abstractly and directly into a judgment. For the material being to be knowable as a thing-in-itself, it must be directly given as a thing-in-itself, and only a sensory faculty can do that. Every attempt to turn the sensory evidence into a rational deduction or induction can only have one result, immediate or mediate, which is to destroy it because it belongs to a different order.

The reason Saint Thomas did not give separate consideration to the problem of the existence of the outside world is because for him all actual existence is individual and singular. As he said again and again, when we grasp the singular as such it is the work of our sense faculty: *id quod cognoscit sensus materialiter et concrete, quod est cognoscere singulare directe;—similitudo quae est in sensu, abstrahitur a re ut ab objecto cognoscibili, et ideo res ipsa per illam similitudinem directe cognoscitur* [what the sense faculty knows materially and concretely, it knows directly as singular—the likeness which is in the senses is abstracted from the thing as from a knowable object, and therefore the thing itself is directly known through that likeness]. Unquestionably the intellect does more and better, since it grasps what is abstractly intelligible, but it has another function: *universale est dum intelligitur, singulare dum sentitur* [the universal is grasped while things are being understood, the singular while they are being sensed]. But the singular is the concretely real. So one must consign the task of solving the problem to *viribus sensitivis quae circa particularia versantur* [to the powers of sense which relate to particular objects].

Descartes' "mathematicism", which forbade him to trust the data of sense, condemned him to rely exclusively on reason, and so to fail. Not that an idealist philosophy will necessarily be incoherent. Quite the contrary. The more idealist it is, the more coherent it will be. The most serious difficulties besetting idealist systems come from the fact that after first declaring they are going to define everything in terms of thought, they then continually keep turning toward things in order to find in them that substance, that "shock", or at least that happening, without which thought would die of vacuity and would not even be able to get itself born.

As for those idealist philosophies which are most rigorously consistent, they are marvelous edifices, magnificent intellectual constructions whose artifice one cannot admire enough, but whose essential fault is their not being attached to reality. Realism can learn from studying them. But it can only do so on condition it remains true to itself, that is to say, by basing itself on the primary evidence which is its raison d'être—the direct grasp of the existence of things in sense perception.

III

The Specific Nature
of the Philosophic Order

Among the reasons for the low esteem in which scholastic philosophy is held today, the most profound, and the one containing most truth, is the scientific sterility of medieval thought and the difficulty there now is in reconciling it with the conclusions of positive science.

That sterility is a fact. It was not a total sterility, as the poorly informed sometimes imagine. In the thirteenth century there were men at the universities of both Paris and Oxford who were aware that a science of nature, either of a purely mathematical type, similar to Cartesian science, or of an empirical kind like Aristotle's, was a possibility, and who yet did not for a moment doubt that such a science could be harmonized with theology. For no doubt complex reasons, the undertaking came to nothing. However that may be, when the truth is faced, there is not a single great scientific discovery one can rightly attribute to the Middle Ages, and even if one managed to attribute some to them, these would be due to isolated initiatives on the part of men whose ideas were not in the mainstream of the thought of their time.

The most important consequence of this fact is that, not having been set in motion by medieval philosophy, the scientific movement of the seventeenth century took place in opposition to it. Apart from the possibly unique case of Leibniz, who was drawn to Aristotle by deep affinities, there are hardly any first-rate minds around the year 1630 who did not feel themselves compelled to make a choice between science with its evidence on the one hand, and scholasticism with its lack of certitudes on the other.

From this point on, what the Middle Ages will be blamed for is not only the practical sterility of its speculative thought, but also, and even more, for its theoretical sterility. The objection is all the more serious because peripatetic philosophy, which was not able to give birth to modern science, fought against it from the moment it was born, combated it in the fields of astronomy, physics, biology, and medicine, and suffered a series of well-deserved defeats, from which it has still not recovered.

Facts like these, in proof of which it would be easy to multiply historical instances, are more than facts; they are symptomatic of certain ideas. If scholasticism was not the mother of modern science, indeed behaved toward it more like a stepmother, it is improbable that this was the result of some kind of historical accident, but rather that it was due to reasons whose nature it is our duty to uncover. The whole question boils down to determining whether its philosophical essence is such that it is incompatible with positive science, as the majority believe to be true, in which case I would not myself hesitate to sacrifice it, or whether on the contrary, as I believe to be true, it only has to become more faithful to its own essence than it was in order to harmonize with science and even help it to develop.

To understand the problem at issue, it is perhaps simplest to go back to the initial data and to find out how the rupture between the Middle Ages and modern thought came about. Since we are studying the question under its philosophical aspect, it is plain that we should turn to a philosopher for an explanation, and none can inform us about it better than René Descartes. When the *Discourse on Method* appeared, it came too late on the scene to kill scholasticism. All the creative forces of contemporary thought had long turned away from it and betaken themselves elsewhere. But it remains true that Descartes drew up the death certificate. To analyze the causes of the death, to show what it was that prevented scholasticism from thinking and so from living, to define the rules of a method productive of new truths because opposed at every point to the old method, was to do much more than turn away from scholasticism. It amounted to suppressing it by supplanting it. However, the manner in which Descartes supplanted it is sufficiently remarkable for us to give it our attention.

All of Cartesianism, and in a sense all of modern thought, goes back to that winter's night in 1619, when, shut up beside a stove in Germany, Descartes conceived the idea of a universal mathematics. From the standpoint we now occupy, the details of the method he will later draw from it are of minor import. What is and remains of capital importance is the spirit of the discovery, and even, for the moment, a single aspect of that spirit.

A young mathematician, fired by his first scientific successes, conceives the possibility, the necessity even, of applying generally to every problem whatsoever the method with which he has just succeeded so brilliantly. Never before had the history of human thought known an extrapolation as vast and bold as that, and it is by it that we still live today.

It drew philosophy into a formidable adventure which, according to the point of view one adopts, can be considered its most decisive advance, or the most serious of the crises it has passed through. The first consequence of Cartesian mathematicism, and the one from which all the others flow, was the obligation it imposed on the philosopher of always going from thought to being, and even of always defining being in terms of ideas or thought. For the mathematician the problem of essence always comes before that of existence; the true circle and the true triangle are the definitions of the circle and of the triangle, while shapes given empirically in sense experience are only approximations in regard to their definitions. It is not by chance that for Descartes, as for Plato, geometry is the science of sciences. Anyhow, the systematic application of the mathematical method to reality could only have as its immediate result the substitution of a limited number of clear ideas, conceived as the true reality, for the concrete complexity of things.

To turn to Descartes' actual experiment, reality, according to this way of looking at things, is reduced to two ideas, and consequently to two substances: thought and extension. And since it is of the nature of ideas to be mutually exclusive, each one comprising whatever makes up its definition and nothing else, it necessarily belongs to the nature of substances to exclude each other, each one comprising whatever enters into its definition and nothing else.

It is difficult to exaggerate the philosophical import of such a reform. Up to Descartes' time, and particularly during the Middle Ages, it had always been agreed that philosophy consisted in a transposition of reality into conceptual terms. In that sense, it is quite fair to characterize it as an abstract conceptualism. But it is not fair to accuse it of having reified its concepts. On the contrary, the scholastic method is and always has been to go from things to concepts, with the result that several concepts are required to express the essence of a single thing, according to the number of the points of view it studies it from, and that no system is less exposed to the danger of taking what it abstracts from reality for reality itself.

To convince oneself of this, one only has to consider any substance one pleases. For the scholastic, a substance is always made up of matter and form, that is to say, of two concepts, although matter is not a thing apart from the form, nor the form a thing apart from the matter. The person who reified concepts was not Saint Thomas but Descartes, and he could not avoid doing so once he raised concepts to the rank of Ideas. He turned abstractions from reality into models of reality, about which it is not enough to say that reality is supposed to conform to them but which are reality itself. On this point the difference between the two philosophies leaps to the eye as soon as one realizes that for Descartes every substance is fully known because it is reducible to the content of its idea, whereas for a scholastic every substance as such is unknown, because it is something other than the sum of the concepts we extract from it.

By turning reality into a mosaic of clear ideas, Cartesian mathematicism raised difficulties which the whole of the seventeenth and eighteenth centuries tried to resolve, and which the nineteenth century finally despaired of resolving, at the same time despairing of philosophy itself. A universe consisting of extension and thought can only be expressed through a specific philosophy, to which corresponds an equally specific science. In the first case we get a pure spiritualism; in the second a pure mechanism. For science, nothing, at first sight, could be more satisfying, and it is all too natural that it should so regard things, since having inspired the method, it is bound to recognize itself in the results. But it is altogether different for philosophy, which, having abdicated the right to a method of its own, has to try and gather philosophical results from a method which does not belong to it.

What Descartes does not tell us is how the domain of pure thought can enter into relations with pure extension, given that it is the characteristic of substances to exclude each other. Having left us with thought (not a soul), and extension (not a body), he does not know how to account for the union of soul and body. When, as a solution, he offers us a third idea, that of a union of soul and body which can be felt but not known, he contradicts his whole method of clear and distinct ideas. The remark of Leibniz remains true: At that point, M. Descartes abandoned the game.

When others after him took up the formidable problem of the "communication of substances" they took it up on the basis of the very positions established by Descartes, and because of this involved themselves in a series of costly hypotheses, each of which, no matter how different from the rest, was in essence an attempt to build a bridge joining together again the segments of reality between which the Cartesian method had dug an uncrossable ditch. As it is by definition impossible to go directly from one to the other, there is nothing astonishing in finding that the bridge has to pass through God. The occasionalism of Malebranche, the pre-established harmony of Leibniz, the parallelism of Spinoza—all are so many metaphysical "epicycles" for resolving a badly propounded problem; the problem is to be solved by saving, with the help of these complementary devices, the very principle which makes it insoluble.

The grand metaphysical systems of the seventeenth century are pure masterpieces, perhaps the most perfectly self-consistent systems of ideas which anyone has ever produced, precisely because, working on pure ideas, as in mathematics, the complexity of reality could in no way inconvenience them. What does inconvenience them is the difficulty of rejoining reality. Having expelled quality from the field of extension, they do not know how to account for it when it reappears in thought. Having begun triumphantly with ideas, they are ultimately unable to explain physical sensation—that low-grade, suspect, even, if one likes, despicable function, in which one nevertheless sees something make its appearance that is not pure thought, since it is not an intelligibility, but which is not extension either, since it is already thought. If, in order to apply a principle, one has to multiply contradictory hypotheses, that is not a proof the principle is false, but it is a sign that it is. One can well make use here of the principle of "economy of thought", so dear to Ernst Mach: when theories involve the inquirer in growing complications, it is time to look for simpler theories and give them preference.

The problem of the communication of substances raised insuperable difficulties as soon as the question arose of passing from one order of substances to another. It was just as difficult passing from one substance to another within a given order, for the difficulty was the same. Malebranche was well aware of the fact, and the reason he resolutely rejected every possibility of a way out, that is to say, all transitive causality in the order of secondary causes, was precisely because, each substance being really distinct from every other substance, the sort of mutual participation in each other's being, which causality is, becomes an impossibility in his system. Leibniz's monad, a simple indivisible entelechy, which in order to exist must be directly created, and directly annihilated if it is to cease to exist, is without "windows through which anything can enter or leave it".

Nothing could be more logical. But the subsequent history of philosophy is no less so. The lesson provided by Malebranche was not lost, and it was David Hume who took it to heart. If we do not understand how one body can act on another body, or one thought on another thought, or a body on a thought, or a thought on a body, we likewise do not understand how even a supreme thought can act on bodies, because all our ideas about God are drawn from our experience, and we could have no idea of God's causality where we had no idea of our own.[1] Hume's skepticism, therefore, descends in a direct line from Cartesian mathematicism. All it does is show the impossibility of re-establishing real relations between substances once one has totally and irrevocably separated them.

After Hume, the only course left to Kant, in order to save a causality no longer possible to find in things, was to conclude that it is prescribed for things by thought. Thus the Cartesian cycle reached completion with the purity of a perfect curve, and according to the demands of its first principle: having started from the mind, philosophy, after several fruitless attempts to escape from it, declared its final resolve to remain there. However, there is no reason to regard this act of resignation as a triumph. It recalls the similar act of resignation made by Descartes when, abandoning the search for ways of prolonging human life, he declared himself content simply to teach men how not to fear dying.

One would be thoroughly deceived were one to imagine that the effects of mathematicism only made themselves felt in the metaphysical order. They impinged on morals, and through them affected sociology. The originator here is no longer Descartes but Thomas Hobbes, whose political philosophy indeed Descartes esteemed much more highly than his metaphysics.[2]

What we are given in reality is a concrete complexity whose elements mutually sustain each other. Man is not only a rational animal; he is also a political animal, because the State is the necessary condition for the perfect development of his

---

[1] D. Hume, *An Inquiry Concerning Human Understanding*, VII, I, ed. L. A. Selby-Bigge, p. 72. The whole tenor of Hume's reasoning in this passage, a capital one for the history of philosophy, is directly and consciously aimed at Malebranche's occasionalism. Hume accepts his critique of transitive causality, but extends the application of it from man to God.

[2] Descartes, Letter of 1643, ed. Adam-Tannery, vol. 4, p. 67, 1.10–26.

rationality. That is why we never come upon the individual except as a member of a State, outside which he could not fully realize his essence or even live, although the State itself never subsists except in individuals, who are its very substance. It is, therefore, equally true to say that one finds nothing in the individual which does not come to him from society, and that there is nothing in society which does not come to it from individuals, because it forms them and they compose it.

In contrast, let us imagine this complex reality split up into ideas, each of which will define a substance. The individual becomes a thing-in-itself, the State a different thing in itself, and the problem of the communication of substances presents itself in a new form, just as insoluble as the first. This is where Hobbes led modern thought by defining men, whether bodily or spiritually, as isolatable and concretely equal individuals.[3] His political Cartesianism set up the individual as a being on his own, and consequently as an end in himself, whose subordination to the State as a higher end became difficult, if not impossible.

From this point on, the political problem becomes what it will remain for Rousseau: finding in the individual, as such, a reason for subordinating him to anything other than himself, which is even more difficult than finding a way of squaring the circle with a ruler and compass. It is clear that for a social atom like the Hobbesian individual, the right of nature is nothing but the liberty to make use of any means he thinks fit for assuring his own welfare.[4] Each man, says the *Leviathan*, has a natural right over every single thing.

[3] Hobbes, *Leviathan*, I, chap. 13. The whole beginning of this chapter is an application to political man of what the beginning of the *Discourse on Method* says of intellectual man. Even some of Descartes' own turns of phrase can be found in it. (The *Leviathan* was published in 1651.)

[4] *Leviathan*, I, chap. 14.

How, after that, and with liberties of this kind, are we going to be able to put together a social body? How are we going to be able to arrange things so that, in the name of my own rights, what belongs to me ceases to belong to me? Hence all the theories of a "social contract", by various devices, struggle to obtain from rights, regarded from the start as absolute, the duty of renouncing themselves, which is tantamount to producing slavery out of a bundle of liberties.

Put in these terms, the problem was so difficult that efforts to solve it inevitably mushroomed. But logically they were bound to lead to the recognition of the contradictory character of the problem and to set these two antinomical realities, which are impossible to reconcile, in hostile opposition. On the one hand, we are given the individual in a pure state; and since the definition of an individual as such is to exist on his own, the outcome is the anarchic individualism of Max Stirner,[5] or the aesthetic individualism of Nietzsche. The Unique Individual and his possessions; nothing could be more logical, and Stirner showed himself a philosopher in being able to reduce an idea to its essence. If the individual is nothing but an individual, it is illogical to make the collectivity from the individual. What is logical is the wholesale elimination of the State as a constraining force. But if, on the other hand, we take the collectivity as such, since its essence is the negation of the individual, it becomes contradictory to build it out of individuals, and in this matter Comte and Durkheim are the true philosophers. "A man is nothing; Humanity is all." Here again everything is coherent, because in a collective being as such, there can be no place for the individual as such; in advance and by

---

[5] See on this point the remarkable work of M. V. Basch, *L'individualisme anarchiste, Max Stirner*, 2nd ed. (Paris: Alcan, 1928).

definition he finds himself eliminated, reduced to nothing, denied existence. Insofar, therefore, as modern society endeavors to reform itself along the lines of its own teachings, it is condemned to oscillate between anarchism and collectivism, or to live empirically by a shameful compromise which can in no way justify itself.

As a phenomenon, the cult of antinomies in modern philosophy has nothing surprising about it. Kant collides with them; Hegel lives by them and thinks that the effort to surmount them is what constitutes philosophy. The whole task of medieval philosophy, on the contrary, was to avoid them. For Saint Thomas and Duns Scotus, the fact that they are harmonized in reality proves that they are not unsurmountable, and that in committing oneself to representing reality as it is, one ought not to come across them. For it is we who introduce them by our mathematicism. If there is a single initial error at the root of all the difficulties philosophy is involved in, it can only be the one Descartes committed when he decreed, a priori, that *the method of one of the sciences of reality was valid for the whole of reality.*

The result of this fatal decision would sooner or later be much more than philosophical difficulties; it would be the disappearance of philosophy itself. Whatever the science may be whose procedures one erects into universal method, one condemns oneself in advance to deriving from that method only what it can give, that is to say, science and not philosophy. Few mathematicians today would accept Descartes' idea that his *Meditations* are, as he flattered himself they were, as certain as mathematics, or even more so. However, in itself, and independently of the difficulties it becomes involved in, a metaphysics of the mathematical type remained a possibility because, in both subjects, thought proceeds by the construction of notions and stays in the order of pure ideas. Cartesian metaphysics can only by a great effort reach the same conclusions as medieval metaphysics—the spirituality of the soul, the existence of God, the existence of matter. Nevertheless, since it ultimately does reach them, it can still be conscious of existing. It is quite otherwise with Kant, for whom the method of Newtonian physics provides the general type. In physics, all knowledge presupposes sensory intuition. If, therefore, other branches of knowledge are judged in terms of their resemblance to physics, knowledge will be absent where sense intuition is lacking. Consequently, it goes without saying that the fate of metaphysics as a science is sealed in advance. Deprived of concepts, it no longer has anything but ideas and finds itself irrevocably trapped in their antinomies.

It is from this point on that, despairing of philosophy as a science, men begin to look for pretexts to justify it in an order other than that of rational knowledge. Kant, who neither wishes to nor can do without metaphysics, tries to ground its conclusions as moral postulates. Comte, who has reduced objective knowledge to scientific knowledge once and for all, but who is also aware of the inevitable anarchy of a purely "empirical" thought, seeks to legitimatize philosophy as a subjective synthesis from the point of view of Humanity. Finally, Bergson, feeling the need of surpassing the scientific order so as to reach the philosophic order, makes an admirable attempt to rejoin intuition beyond the concept. But that intuition is an *experience* rather than a *knowledge* of the real, an everlastingly fertile method of investigation rather than a formula for discoveries, and while it gives us the means for criticizing science when it mistakes itself for philosophy, it does not give us the means for constructing a philosophy.[6] For in order to make progress in

---

[6] The pragmatism of James, a more complicated but less philosophical enterprise, endeavors to drown both science and philosophy in the common category

philosophy, it may indeed be necessary to achieve and repeatedly recover contact with the unexpressed; nevertheless, in spite of deficiencies of expression which must be ceaselessly corrected, philosophy consists in what it is able to say about the unexpressed.

One should not, therefore, be too surprised today to see philosophy resigned to committing suicide and regarding its resignation as a triumph. From the method of any science one can only derive what belongs to that science, and whatever in other sciences is reducible to it. From the methods of all the sciences taken together, one can draw only an ensemble of sciences, which is fine enough, but would leave no room for an autonomous philosophy. Following this path, one necessarily ends up either with the absolute positivism of a Littré, which reduces the content of philosophy to that of science, pure and simple, or with the idealism of L. Brunschvicg, who reduces philosophy to a critical reflection on the stages traversed by human thought in the building up of science, in other words, to a history of the Mind.

So here we have philosophy in a state where it seems difficult for it to go any further on the road to its own dissolution. But as the last step on the journey out is also the first step on the way home, this is perhaps the place to stop and think again in preparation for a new departure.

To start with, any thought of returning to medieval philosophy seems in the highest degree absurd. It was medieval philosophy which lived on painfully in the dogmatic metaphysics of the seventeenth century. When science eliminated all metaphysics, scholasticism was what it succeeded in eliminating. After three centuries of scientific progress, that very progress which relegated the world of Aristotle to

---

of the advantageously workable. In order to save philosophy, he made two victims instead of one.

the world of fantasy, how could there be any question of returning to it?

There is no such question, and not only for reasons of expediency which, however pressing, would have nothing to do with philosophy. The scientific sterility of the Middle Ages has to be condemned for the same reasons which make it necessary today to condemn the philosophic sterility of scientism. Aristotle, too, exaggerated the scope of a particular science and the value of its method to the detriment of others. In a sense he was more blameworthy than Descartes, because he was thereby openly contradicting the demands of his own method, whereas Descartes merely followed the demands of his method. All the same, Aristotle's error was philosophically less dangerous because it was an error of fact and left the rights of philosophy intact. In biologizing inorganic nature, Aristotle and the medieval philosophers condemned themselves to ignorance about the sciences of the inorganic world, whose present popularity stems above all from the inexhaustible practical fruitfulness they have given proof of. But the total mathematization of knowledge, in practice and principle, had a strangely limiting effect on physics and chemistry and made biology, metaphysics, and consequently morals impossible. This is the point I have still to discuss.

For a realist philosopher, thought has no other content apart from what its faculties allow it to abstract from things and which it elaborates, thanks to its principles. He sees nothing abnormal in this proceeding, all the more so because in the Middle Ages he was a Christian, and the Christian world being a creation of God, not of man, Christian philosophy spontaneously views problems from the perspective of the object. No doubt every medieval philosopher would readily have granted to Descartes that the sciences, taken together, are but the human mind, which is always one and the same no matter how many problems it applies itself to. But if the human mind considered in itself is always one, the things it applies itself to are not, and that is why its ways of approaching reality should be diversified like reality itself. An Aristotelian discourse on *the* method is therefore an impossibility. One can speak, in the Aristotelian context, only of a discourse on *methods*. The mathematical method corresponds with the order of abstract quantity; even so it has to diversify itself according to whether it is dealing with continuous or discontinuous quantity, with geometry or with arithmetic. The physical order has its method, because it has to study the movement and properties of inorganic bodies. The biological order requires still another method, because it tackles the study of organized beings, and so on for psychology, morality, and sociology. It would be quite wrong to consider these different methods as isolated, because the method of a more abstract science governs those of the more concrete sciences and extends over their territory; but they are specific methods which remain distinct in as much as each order of reality, by reason of its separateness, requires an appropriate mode of investigation. Thus Wisdom, or first philosophy, or metaphysics, establishes the principles which regulate all the other sciences, and, humanly speaking, depends on none of them. As the others study the various modes of being, she [wisdom] studies being in itself, in its essence and in its properties. It is the science of being as being. Mathematics is the science of quantity; physics is the science of mobile being; biology that of living being; psychology that of being which knows; and sociology that of the human being living in society. There could not be a more comprehensive and flexible approach, and a priori one does not see why a philosophy which adopted it should have failed to give a proper interpretation of any of the orders of reality.

There was nothing fore-ordained about the failure. Aristotle's error was not remaining faithful to his principle—a science of reality for each order of reality; medieval philosophy's mistake was copying his error. Making a blunder of the opposite kind to Descartes', Aristotle established the biological method as the method for physics. It is generally agreed that the only branches of positive knowledge in which Aristotelianism has been responsible for some progress are those connected with morphology and the functions of living creatures. This is because Aristotle was first and foremost a naturalist, just as Descartes was first and foremost a mathematician—so much so that instead of, like Descartes, reducing the organic to the inorganic, he claimed to understand the inorganic in terms of the organic. Struck by the dominant role of form in the living creature, he made it not only a principle for explaining the phenomena of life, but extended it beyond living beings to mobile beings in general. This was the origin of the famous theory of substantial forms, which it was Descartes' first concern to get rid of. For a scholastic, indeed, physical bodies are endowed with forms to which they owe both their movement and their properties; and just as the soul is a certain kind of form, that of something living, form is a certain kind of soul, a kind which the forms of inorganic beings and the forms or souls of organized beings both belong to.

This is what explains the relative sterility of scholastic philosophy in the field of physics and even in that of chemistry, and at the same time the inadequacy of Cartesianism in the field of the biological sciences. If there is something more in a living being than a pure mechanism, Descartes is bound in advance to miss it. But if that which defines the living thing as such is not to be found in physics, scholasticism will not only fail to find it, but will never discover what actually is to be found there. Moreover, in looking for it in physics, scholasticism will have wasted its time, and because it was convinced that all the operations of inorganic bodies are explainable in terms of forms, it fought with all its might against those who claimed to see something else in them, clung obstinately to its impossible case, and in losing it was itself ruined. Three centuries spent in classifying what can be measured—as today people sometimes obstinately insist on measuring what should be classified[7]—produced nothing but a pseudo-physics as dangerous for the future of science as for that of philosophy, which imagined itself linked to that pseudo-physics. Thus, scholasticism did not know how to draw from its principles the physics which could and should flow from them.

So our first duty today is to be more faithful to the demands of realism than the Middle Ages were, and giving each order of reality its due.

In each order, the reality of the form should be preserved, since without it one cannot account for structures, and it remains the principle of reality's intelligibility. Insofar as it determines the end to which energies are directed and the conditions of their processes, it everywhere requires mechanics, imposing on physical or chemical forces structural laws which diversify bodies and maintain a real distinction between those energies. There is more reason still for the reality of the form to fulfill this role in botany

[7] It is plain that Aristotle's error, though less serious than Descartes' from the philosophical point of view, was more serious from the point of view of science. Extending the principles of a more general science over a less general one, as Descartes did, at least leaves the door open to reaching in the latter what they have in common with the former—whence the possible, if always partial, mechanization of biology. But making the method of a more specialized science flow back over a more generalized one results in depriving the latter of its object. So, in missing the proper object of physics and chemistry, Aristotle missed at the same time everything biochemistry can tell us about the biological order, which, though neither the sum of what is to be learned about it nor the most important part, is perhaps the most useful. Here he was guilty not only of a grave theoretical oversight but also of a practical one, something which human utilitarianism will never forgive him for.

and zoology, where *types* are even more manifestly facts and laws. Indeed, *typology* is an absolutely universal scientific problem. It is just as necessary for the study of the inorganic world as for that of the organic, and although the actual orientation of the sciences is directed elsewhere, its factual reality remains. It will always have to be kept in mind, and the form is the only principle which explains it.

We are not therefore required to get rid of the hylomorphism of inorganic beings, but what seems to be needed is a clear distinction between the notion of organic form and that of inorganic form. *Formae naturales sunt actuosae et quasi vivae* [natural forms are active and quasi–living], said the Scholastics. Between Cartesian "artificialism", which turned animals into machines, and Aristotelian vitalism, which treated physical bodies as if they were animals, it should be possible to find room for mechanism in the physical order and vitalism in the biological. Every "nature" requires a formal principle, but not every form is a living form.[8] Although the

---

[8] It is indeed certain that in spite of the error of imagination, which persuaded the scholastics to think of the forms of inorganic beings as resembling the forms of living beings, hylomorphism keeps all its value. One only has to recall that metaphysical notions come to birth when the mind, on making contact with facts about our material universe of the most general kind, carries out an act of judgment in the light of its knowledge of being, that is to say, in the light of the principle of contradiction, and that in consequence such a notion is analogical, like the notion of being itself. The concept of form is a notion of this kind, being realized differently in inorganic and living beings. But as the human mind never engages in thought without calling on the imagination and sensory experience, the reason is naturally tempted with metaphysical, and consequently analogical, concepts to link each to a single univocal mental image or object of sense. Aristotle was yielding to an attraction of this kind, his medical education being responsible for his wholesale "biologizing" of form. However, we should note in his defense that, when one recalls book 6 of his *Physics* and certain passages of books 2 and 7, it is apparent he had glimpsed the role of quantity and measure in scientific knowledge. If he did not follow this path any further, his ignorance of mathematics, of which he only seems to have known the basic elements,

inorganic form is a principle which determines structures and regulates energies, it is not a source of energy that can be calculated or experimentally demonstrated; it is not a spontaneous internal power whose effects would manifest themselves as observable quantitative variations.

But at the same time it is apparent that the failure of medieval physics leaves the value of its philosophy untouched, and even in a sense confirms its value, since that philosophy miscarried only through not being faithful enough to its principles. Nothing ties it to Ptolemy's astronomy, to geocentrism, to explaining the movements of heavenly bodies by the propulsive power of heavenly intelligences. It has no obligation to believe with Saint Thomas that bodies receive from their substantial forms a predetermined inclination toward a particular spot, or that the reflection and refraction of light rays are metaphors of a corporeal kind to express immaterial realities. No one is so wrong-headed as not to recognize that what is false is false. Not only does all this scientific rubbish deserve to collapse, as it has already collapsed, but everything in the metaphysical and psychological order based on it necessarily collapses with it. Therefore, a revaluation of the medieval tradition must start with its principles, not in order to decide in advance what results they can or cannot give, but to put them freely to the test in order to discover their value as a means of explaining reality and to see how far it extends. The problem is not to involve them in new systems, with whose outworn elements they would eventually seem once again linked, but to revive them in their enduring purity and fruitfulness, if only to ensure that spiritual goods which ought to be permanent acquisitions for us are not thrown away and lost.

---

perhaps explains why. This fact may well have had a considerable influence on the general orientation of his work.

The first and most necessary of those goods is the existence of a philosophy which is truly an autonomous discipline of the mind, and of a metaphysics to crown it. The old definition of philosophy, as Auguste Comte finally recognized, remains true: it is the study of wisdom. It therefore embraces all the sciences together, each of which strives to perfect the instrument adapted to the order of reality it has undertaken to explain. But over and above the problems which the different modes of being raise, there is the problem raised by being itself, not, how do such and such things exist, but what is existence? In what does it consist? Why is there existence at all, seeing that the existence we directly know does not seem to have in itself a sufficient reason for its existence? Is it necessary or contingent? And if it is contingent, does it not postulate a necessary existence as its cause and explanation?

Such then is the object of the final and highest science that the human mind ascends to in the order of purely natural knowledge: the science of existence over and above the sciences dealing with the modes of existence. This science, called "metaphysics", which the Greeks founded, clearly seeing its necessity, Christian philosophy will never allow to perish. That is because it is the first and only science which saw and still sees the very existence of beings as contingent, that is to say, as also requiring their own principle of explanation—whose nature has to be studied by a science distinct from the other sciences, and which governs them because its object is the problem without which there would be no other problem to propound. As long as Christianity lasts there will be metaphysics in order to join the diverse modes of existence to Him *qui non aliquo modo est, sed est, est* [Who does not exist in a particular way, but Who simply and solely is]. Each science has its place, but above all the others is the science of that without which there would be no science because there would be neither reality to know nor intelligence to grasp it.

IV

The Realist Method

I have tried to show first of all why and in what sense it is possible to speak of a methodical realism, in order to define an attitude which I believe to be in agreement with the Aristotelian tradition and also to be philosophically sound. I am not here concerned with the question whether we ought to accept Aristotle's psychology in all its structural and technical details, but with something quite different. The problem I am discussing is that of our basic philosophical attitude.

Now it seems to me that today, on just this point, we are in a state of not having made up our minds, which may be convenient, but which, if we genuinely want to undertake philosophy, we absolutely must get away from. The truth is that realism is not properly presented. Most of our contemporaries think that, at bottom, being a philosopher and adopting an idealist method are one and the same thing. When idealism is aware of its nature and of the principles which determine it, such an attitude is consistent. What is inconsistent and dangerous is that ill-defined idealism, adopted as a matter of course, which surrounds us today. When someone calls himself an idealist, what does he really mean by it?

Since the problem under discussion is the elementary one of the existence of the outside world, a pure idealism would in the first place be one that reduced reality to a *percipere* or a *percipi*. This point of view, which is fairly close to Berkeley's, would reduce reality to the "apprehended" and to our apprehension of the "apprehended". The universe, being composed entirely of thoughts and images, would contain neither matter nor substances endowed with an existence of their own independent of the act that knows them. In this sense, the world would not only be contemporaneous with thought, but would be confounded with it and have no other existence than that of thought. It would be easy enough to find statements by present-day philosophers, and even certain scientists, which presuppose belief in a doctrine of this kind. "Thought is nothing but a flash of lightning in a long night, but the lightning flash is everything", and "the scientist's thought creates the scientific fact", may be brilliant as dicta and their effect is plain enough. But what are they supposed to mean? Anyone who wants thought to be *everything* must be ready to agree that outside thought there is *nothing*; also that, as a consequence, there was nothing before thought, and that, if thought were to disappear, there would be nothing after it. In a word, when the problem is presented like this, one must face the fact that being, because limited to the content of knowledge, is in itself inseparable from it.

If one goes to this extreme, though one may be wrong, at least one cannot be accused of inconsistency. Unfortunately, however, those who make use of these maxims do not really accept what they imply. They would be most reluctant to state that the world we live in did not exist before the appearance on it of the lowest organisms capable of feeling; indeed, they teach just the opposite as an established scientific fact. It would be difficult to get them to say that physics is nature itself, rather than a science of nature; that the scientist does not study things, but confers existence on them by a special creative power of the mind; that to observe a fact is the same as drawing it out of nothingness. On the contrary, they nearly all agree in recognizing that, on the one hand, the inorganic world preceded by aeons the organic and sensitive world, whose existence it conditions, and that, on the other hand, science is constantly at grips with something given, which continually obliges it to revise already established theories and systems.

It is a characteristic of thought to be faced by what is opaque; as soon as that wall of opaqueness becomes translucent, there is always a similar one behind it; and this barrier, which thought strikes against with such a beneficial and fruitful impact, appears to it as the very opposite of a free decree or law of the spirit. The way things actually occur suggests that, by means of science, thought progressively assimilates what is intelligible in a world given to it from without, not that it creates both the intelligibility and existence of that world. We are therefore, at this point, faced with making a choice, which is both free and necessary. We are free to choose whichever option we like, but if we are philosophers, we are compelled to make a choice of some sort. When a man calls himself an idealist, does he mean—yes or no—that the being of the universe is reduced to that of thought? If yes, we might as well rejoin Berkeley and, along with him, reduce the world to the language spoken by the Author of nature to mere spirits. At least his position has the merit of straightforwardness. If the answer is no, what do people mean when calling themselves idealists?

Probably they have in mind an alternative idea; they are saying, in other words, that they are critical philosophers, partisans of the critical idealism of Kant. Here again there are two ways of being such partisans, one which is consistent, the other not. In essence, critical philosophy is not a metaphysics but a method, a method indeed which excludes in advance the possibility of all metaphysical dogmatism. To

ask oneself with Kant on what conditions a pure a priori
physics is possible and pose the problem from the transcen-
dental point of view is to banish from the realm of true knowledge every discipline whose initial conditions differ from those
of Newtonian physics. Metaphysics and morals belong to
this category. At first sight, such a decision can well seem
arbitrary and people are right to ask themselves whether the
critical method is not rather too uncritical. However that
may be, it is in no way contradictory, nor is it impossible—
only one must be ready to stand by the consequences.

In my opinion, the first and most important of these consequences is that critical philosophy has a binding duty not
to turn itself into a metaphysics, under pain of betraying its
own essence. Critical philosophy, therefore, has absolutely
nothing to say about the problem we are concerned with,
since that has to do with being and is essentially a metaphysical one. Kant himself seems to have realized this. The
problem which all students of philosophy put to their
instructors—if Kant is really a critical philosopher, how can
he know there are things-in-themselves; by what right does
he make use of the category of causality to establish their
existence?—clearly shows the persistent independence in Kant
of the metaphysical and critical points of views. As a metaphysician, he won't have any of Berkeley's idealism, but posits a world of substances independent of thought. This initial
decision owes nothing to his critical method. It neither confirms nor invalidates the method in any way because it is
made beforehand. In this sense, L. Brunschvicg, who clearly
sees what the essence of critical philosophy implies when it
is taken in its absolute purity, has rightly said that "it is not
certain, it cannot in any case be proved, that what the nature
of the method neglects, is in fact negligible."

Nothing could be more true. But then one must stick to
one's viewpoint. When one has laid down once and for all

that, for us, nature is by definition identical with the activity of the mind, one should not subsequently forget that one has given up the right to inquire whether or not there is such a thing as nature outside the mind, and if there is, what is its possible relationship with the mind. One no longer has the right to talk about the "shock" it gives the mind, since the problem of knowing whether there is a nature has not been posed and remains by definition outside the domain of critical philosophy. Still less has one the right to talk about consciousness as though it entered into relations with a datum endowed with its own reality and whose secret it could busy itself with unfolding. Nevertheless, this is what our critical philosophers never cease doing. Placing themselves from the start outside the confines of metaphysics, they pass judgment on metaphysical idealism and realism, as if both were subject to their jurisdiction. Worse still, they allow themselves without more ado the benefit of metaphysical realism in order to supplement and give some body to their critical idealism, which indeed badly needs it—in doing so, of course, they act with good sense. Kant was quite right to posit things-in-themselves; Brunschvicg is also right to talk about nature and the "shock" the mind receives from it. The only thing is that, in doing so, they ought to admit that they are granting themselves an outside world (which I congratulate them for doing), while at the same time refusing to make a frank admission of their realism (which I cannot congratulate them for doing).

All this amounts to saying that behind every critical philosopher there is a metaphysician, often a realist metaphysician, who fails to recognize himself, shuts his eyes to his own existence, and refuses to let others take cognizance of theirs. Yet the latter is all the realist claims to be doing. He is simply someone who takes account of his own position and publicly avows it, on his own behalf and that of some others. What then exactly is his position?

Essentially, it consists in a considered choice between two possible methods, Aristotle's and Descartes'. Either one begins with being, in which thought is included *ab esse ad nosse valet consequentia* [from a thing's reality one can be certain of its possibility], or one starts from thought, in which being is included *a posse ad esse valet consequentia* [from its possibility one cannot be certain of its reality]. As the forerunner of Kant, Descartes chose a particular science as the model for knowledge in general. The difference between them is that instead of choosing physics he chose mathematics, to which he reduces physics. They resemble each other in that, anticipating Kant, Descartes transformed a method into a metaphysics. He still regarded metaphysics as a science, which was no longer possible for Kant, because if mathematics is chosen as the model science, a science of metaphysics remains possible. In contrast, if physics provides the model, metaphysics lacks the sensory intuition necessary for its constitution as a science. Consequently, Descartes, who thought as a mathematician, was able to persuade himself that an idealist method not only would not suppress metaphysics, but would on the contrary place it on an unshakeable foundation.

The outcome is well known. If one regards Cartesianism as a metaphysics, it ends in Berkeley's idealism; but when one regards it as a purely methodical idealism, it results in the critical idealism of Kant. So one can either begin with Descartes, provided one accepts in advance the consequences implicit in Cartesianism, or one stays in the daylight of essences and consequently in philosophy. But if one decides to start with Descartes and finish with Aristotle, and to employ an idealist method while shamelessly making use of a reality one has no right to, one brings confusion into the heart of philosophy and makes its cultivation impossible. To make it possible again is the reason why realists are realists and call themselves such. They too follow a method, but they do not lay down *beforehand* what that method is to be, as though it were a necessary pre-condition for their philosophy. Instead, they find their method *in* their philosophy. So they never have to ask themselves whether it is legitimate to transform their method into a metaphysics, because their method is that metaphysics, which is fully aware of its proceedings, of its initial positions, and of their implications.

The fundamental principle of realism, when it defines itself in relation to idealism, whether metaphysical or critical, is that because all existence is given to me through an act of knowledge, it does not in the least follow that my act of knowledge is the cause of that existence. In all idealism there is an initial postulate which can be tolerated as long as it presents itself only as a postulate, but which, when it offers itself as evidence, too easily becomes a sophism. The fact that everything is given me in thought in no way permits me to assert that everything is reducible to thought. It is embarrassing to have to recall these rather elementary points. It can't be avoided, however, because so many people today take it as a manifest and indisputable first principle that realism is an impossible position, and one which is in essence self-contradictory. The truth, on the contrary, is that idealism is a pure and simple postulate which nothing justifies, and whose consequences are such that very few who posit it at the start remain faithful to it later. I am not here discussing the difficulties which turn up later. All I am saying is that the idealism's starting point has neither the evidence of an axiom nor the value of a principle. There is no reason why we should not start by making knowledge an aspect of being rather than being an aspect of knowledge.

I maintain, therefore, that just as there is in Cartesianism a methodical idealism, the kind that starts with *nosse*, there can be a methodical realism, the kind that starts with *esse*.

As long as one makes some kind of conscious state, whether a "passive sensation" or an "apprehended", come before reality, one will remain more or less in debt to the idealist method. The realist method pursues an exactly opposite course. Every given reality implies the thought which apprehends it. Therefore being is the condition of knowing; knowing is not the condition of being. When this has been established, another step in the direction of metaphysics can be taken.

Once it has been granted that the realist position is possible, and when the kind of interdict which idealism tries to impose on it has been lifted, it immediately becomes clear that the relationship of the method to the philosophy in realism is quite different from what it is in idealism. It is not all that easy to escape from reality, and the world had to wait for centuries before thought contemplated this form of suicide. There was only one way it could do it: by laying down a method, stretching reality on it as on a bed of Procrustes, and lopping off whatever projected beyond it. That is why all idealism assumes that a particular method can be autonomous and all-sufficient, and regards it as a thing-in-itself anterior to philosophy, as the rule, pre-condition, and cause of that philosophy. It is also why, when the idealist comes to define reality, he finds himself compelled to hypostatize the method and substitute it for reality. It is no longer enough for the method to explain reality. It must constitute reality, so that it can have the right to deny the existence in any datum of whatever its essence forbids it to find there.

With realism, it is altogether different. Here reality is what dictates the method, and not the method which defines reality. The first thing we know gives us simultaneously the nature of that thing and the means of knowing what knowledge is. Certainly there is nothing to prevent us from imagining a universe where things would happen otherwise. The plain fact is, however, that in the universe we live in, this is the way things actually do happen. In a Cartesian universe, thoughts would first of all have to think themselves, then—descending step by step from their essences to their concepts, from their concepts to their sense impressions, from their sense impressions to their objects—at least by this centrifugal path rejoin the outside world. If things really were like this, idealism would be the natural philosophy of the human mind. We all know that it is not. There is no such thing as a "naïve idealism"; there is not even a natural idealism. From Plato to Descartes, every idealist method has been obliged to explain the existence of realism as the consequence of some kind of original sin. Since realism is manifestly natural, if one wishes to get rid of it, the only way is by proving that nature is corrupt, that what looks like being is not being, and that the testimony of sense intuition, whose immediate evidence seems the most natural and irresistible, is a constant source of illusions and errors.

Realism does not reject the idea of a critique of the different *kinds of knowledge*. It accepts it; it calls for it. But it does reject all a priori critique of *knowledge* as such. Instead of prescribing limits to reason a priori, which soon become limits to reality itself, realism accepts reality in toto and measures our knowledge by the rule of reality. Nothing that is validly known would be so if its object did not first exist—to which we can add that there is nothing to prevent us from seeking to define, within this real order, the relations between the thinker and the thing thought about.

The first thing offered us is the concept of a being thought about by the intellect, and given us in a sensory intuition. If the being, insofar as it can be conceived, is the first object of the intellect, that is because it is directly perceived: *res sunt, ergo cogito* [things are, therefore I think]. We start by perceiving an existence which is given us in itself and not first of all in relation to ourselves. Later, on inquiring into the conditions which make such a fact possible, we realize that the birth of the *concept* presupposes the fertilization of the intellect by the reality which it apprehends. Before truth comes the thing that is true; before judgment and reality are brought into accord, there is the living accord of the intellect with reality; it is because the intellect becomes the real thing that it can afterward conceive its essence. But this realist metaphysics is itself only an interpretation, coming after the initial sensory evidence, of that entering into us of the thing which we call a sensation. So first we have the immediate experience of a thing-in-itself, in which the self of the subject, by an effort of reflection, afterward redis- covers itself. The realist method of reflection starts with the whole in order to distinguish the parts. It will not allow one of the parts, the last of those it reaches, to be posited as the pre-condition for the existence of everything else.

This does not mean that the realist feels no interest in the idealist's efforts to start with a part and then restrict the whole to the part because he cannot get the whole outside the part. All he asks is that the idealist should play his role properly right to the end, and he asks the same of realists. It is not exactly what either of them do. We are constantly coming across realists who begin as idealists, and idealists who end as realists. How could they possibly agree? Each sees the other's inconsistency, but fails to see his own. What I want is an honest disagreement. That is much better than the present confusion, and it is the masters of medieval thought who can help us to get out of it because their position is so clear. Starting as realists, they finished as real- ists. Why should we not go back to the classic way of pre- senting the problem? Because it means going back to the

Middle Ages? It means returning to something much older than that, and perhaps means a return to truth.

Something outside thought would indeed be unthinkable were it not that certain thoughts are acts of knowledge, and that every act of knowledge implies a something beyond thought. What a deliverance it would be for us if we could recognize the elementary truth that the object of epistemology is not *thought*, which is only the consciousness of an act of knowledge, but *knowledge* itself, which is the grasp of an object. All realism implies an analysis of knowledge; all idealism derives from the analysis of a thought. That is why the first duty which the realist method imposes on us is to refuse a hearing to false problems and false sciences, as one of its greatest merits is that it can deliver us from them.

I have said that a realist critique of knowledge is like a squared circle, and even worse. I feel in duty bound to keep on saying it. A critique of knowledge is an enterprise of a special kind which one can only engage in under certain clearly defined conditions. It makes its historical appearance at the moment when idealism, having decided once and for all not to begin with being, asked itself what it was going to do with the transcendentals. Once the true is no longer being as known by the mind, what is truth? Once the good is no longer being as the object of desire, what is the good? And, consequently, what are science and morality? It was at this point that the good, the true, and the beautiful began to transform themselves into *values*, because values are simply transcendentals that strive to subsist after they have severed their connection with being. But from the moment they no longer *are*, it becomes necessary to *ground* them. This is the origin of that sterile proliferation of purely verbal speculation, which encumbers modern philosophy, about values and their foundation; or we should rather say, about their foundation alone, since owing to the fact that these foundations are never discovered, no one ever has time to arrive at the values themselves.

One of the most serious obstacles delaying the flowering of a renewed realism is precisely the illusion that realism's first duty is to develop its own critique of knowledge, and its own epistemological, aesthetic, or moral axiology. Our duty, on the contrary, is to recognize that following such a course would be chasing the shadow of a shadow, since it would entail searching for the foundations of a value which it is only so necessary to ground because values come into being at the very moment these aspects of reality try to take the place of reality itself. Realism is a form of knowing that reaches a knowledge of the self only *in* and through being. It analyzes and endeavors to understand the structure of the reality of which it is a part, and in the midst of which it discovers itself. At the start, it not only finds at its disposal things and its knowledge of those things; it also finds in them—in the progressive knowledge it acquires of these things and of the intellect which knows them—the principles which determine what knowledge is. For the realist, the only principle which can determine the way things ought to be is the essence which causes them to be what they are.

Idealism is completely different. It will not be pacified by our yielding to its claim that philosophy must begin with a study of our faculties of knowledge, and that only by careful examination can we tell the difference between knowledge and illusion. A "critique of knowledge" is neither a reflective analysis of the act of knowledge in which justice would be done to both subject and object, nor is it a "critique of the branches of knowledge" which would try to show what are the signs by which the true can be distinguished from the false. It is something else, a something which differs *essentially* from anything realism can undertake. It is an enterprise whose purpose is to give our knowledge an a priori foundation by restricting it.

The problem of grounding knowledge or morality only becomes an obligation when realism is abandoned, and has no meaning as long as one is careful to remain firmly planted in realism. A critique of the faculty of knowledge is an attempt to find in that faculty itself the necessary and sufficient conditions for knowledge, that is to say, to limit the scope of our knowledge to what it itself gives, excluding in advance the hypothesis that it can receive anything from outside. The idealist, therefore, has to ground knowledge, and genuinely tries to, precisely because, having started by emptying knowledge of the object which governs it, he still has to find a meaning for the word truth.

Thus, a critical realism would be acceptable for the idealist insofar as it rid the notion (if it is a notion) of anything that suggested it was aiming at a realist critique of knowledge. That is hardly possible. If *critical realism* means anything, it can only be "critical realism insofar as it remains realism", in other words, a philosophy which goes from being to knowing, while seeking through knowing the a priori conditions of being. If that is not what the term implies, it will no longer signify a realism which is critical, and then what will it mean? We know what *critical idealism* means; it is an idealism whose very essence is to be critical because, at least according to its initial intentions, it refuses to be an empirical idealism. We can go further and say, with a present-day exponent of this doctrine, that "idealism holds all metaphysics to be synonymous with the theory of knowledge"; that is why it is critical. Since the essence of realism is to reject such a position, in what sense can it be critical? I confess; I fail to see how it can be.

Naturally, a realist philosopher, once established in his realism, does not imagine himself at liberty to indulge in an uncritical acceptance of the concepts and judgments he forms on contact with experience. But that is an altogether different question. Saint Thomas had the most incisive of critical faculties, yet he was a realist; subsequently, he was a realist gifted in the highest degree with a critical sense; but he was never a "critical realist", because if he had tried to become "critical", his realism would have ceased to exist. It seems to me evidence of the plainest kind that had his realism ceased to exist, his metaphysics would have ceased to exist too, and that we can only re-establish metaphysics today by returning to realism pure and simple. But we shall only succeed insofar as we reject all compromise with idealism, and first of all with its method, because the method is idealism itself, and as soon as realism gives way to it, it is condemned in advance to lose one by one all its positions. Let us then be utterly plain again. *I think* is evidence, but it is not the primary evidence, which is why we get nowhere if we make it our starting point. That *things exist* is also evidence, the first in order of all the evidence there is, which leads on the one hand to science and on the other to metaphysics. Any sound method will, therefore, take it for its starting point.

V

A Handbook for Beginning Realists

1. The first step on the realist path is to recognize that one has always been a realist; the second is to recognize that, however hard one tries to think differently, one will never manage to; the third is to realize that those who claim they think differently, think as realists as soon as they forget to act a part. If one then asks oneself why, one's conversion to realism is all but complete.

2. Most people who say and think they are idealists would like, if they could, not to be, but believe that is impossible. They are told they will never get outside their thought and that a something beyond thought is unthinkable. If they listen to this objection and look for an answer to it, they are lost from the start, because all idealist objections to the realist position are formulated in idealist terms. So it is hardly surprising that the idealist always wins. His questions invariably imply an idealist solution to problems. The realist, therefore, when invited to take part in discussions on what is not his own ground, should first of all accustom himself to saying no, and not imagine himself in difficulties because he is unable to answer questions which are in fact insoluble, but which for him do not arise.

3. We must begin by distrusting the term "thought"; for the greatest difference between the realist and the idealist is that the idealist thinks, whereas the realist knows. For the realist, thinking simply means organizing knowledge or reflecting on its content. It would never occur to him to make thought the starting point of his reflections, because for him a thought is only possible where there is first of all knowledge. The idealist, however, because he goes from thought to things, cannot know whether what he starts from corresponds with an object or not. When, therefore, he asks the realist how, starting from thought, one can rejoin the object, the latter should instantly reply that it is impossible, and also that this is the principal reason for not being an idealist. Since realism starts with knowledge, that is, with an act of the intellect which consists essentially in grasping an object, for the realist the question does not present an insoluble problem, but a pseudoproblem, which is something quite different.

4. Every time the idealist calls on us to reply to the questions raised by thought, one can be sure that he is speaking in terms of the Mind. For him, Mind is what thinks, just as for us the intellect is what knows. One should therefore, insofar as one can, have as little as possible to do with the term. This is not always easy, because it has a legitimate meaning, but we are living at a time when it has become absolutely necessary to retranslate into realist language all the terms which idealism has borrowed from us and corrupted. An idealist term is generally a realist term denoting one of the spiritual antecedents to knowledge, now considered as generating its own content.

5. The knowledge the realist is talking about is the lived and experienced unity of an intellect with an apprehended reality. This is why a realist philosophy has to do with the thing itself that is apprehended, and without which there would be no knowledge. Idealist philosophers, on the other hand, since they start from thought, quickly reach the point of choosing science or philosophy as their object. When an idealist genuinely thinks as an idealist, he perfectly embodies the essence of a "professor of philosophy", whereas the realist, when he genuinely thinks as a realist, conforms himself to the authentic essence of a philosopher; for a philosopher talks about things, while a professor of philosophy talks about philosophy.

6.　Just as we do not have to go from thought to things (knowing that the enterprise is impossible), neither do we have to ask ourselves whether something beyond thought is thinkable. A something beyond *thought* may well be unthinkable, but it is certain that all *knowledge* implies a something beyond thought. The fact that this something-beyond-thought is given us by knowledge only *in* thought does not prevent it being a something beyond. But the idealist always confuses "being which is given in thought" with "being which is given by thought". For anyone who starts from knowledge, a something beyond thought is so obviously thinkable that this is the only kind of thought for which there can be a beyond.

7.　The realist is committing an error of the same kind if he asks himself how, starting from the self, he can prove the existence of a non-self. For the idealist, who starts from the self, this is the normal and, indeed, the only possible way of putting the question. The realist should be doubly distrustful: first, because he does not start from the self; secondly, because for him the world is not a non-self (which is a nothing), but an in-itself. A thing-in-itself can be given through an act of knowledge. A non-self is what reality is reduced to by the idealist and can neither be grasped by knowledge nor proved by thought.

8. Equally, one should not let oneself be troubled by the classic idealist objection to the possibility of reaching a thing-in-itself, and above all to having true knowledge about it. You define true knowledge, the idealist says, as an adequate copy of reality. But how can you know that the copy reproduces the thing as it is in itself, seeing that the thing is only given to you in thought. The objection has no meaning except for idealism, which posits thought before being, and finding itself no longer able to compare the former with the latter, wonders how anyone else can. The realist, on the contrary, does not have to ask himself whether things do or do not conform to his knowledge of them, because for him knowledge consists in his assimilating his knowledge to things. In a system where the bringing of the intellect into accord with the thing, which the judgment formulates, presupposes the concrete and lived accord of the intellect with its objects, it would be absurd to expect knowledge to guarantee a conformity without which it would not even exist.

9. We must always remember that the impossibilities in which idealism tries to entangle realism are the inventions of idealism. When it challenges us to compare the thing known with the thing-in-itself, it merely manifests the internal sickness, which consumes it. For the realist there is no "noumenon" as the realist understands the term. Since knowledge presupposes the presence to the intellect of the thing itself, there is no reason to assume, behind the thing in thought, the presence of a mysterious and unknowable duplicate, which would be the thing of the thing in thought. Knowing is not apprehending a thing as it is in thought, but, in and through thought, apprehending the thing as it is.

10. To be able to conclude that we must necessarily go from thought to things, and cannot proceed otherwise, it is not enough to assert that everything is given in thought. The fact is, we do proceed otherwise. The awakening of the intelligence coincides with the apprehension of things, which, as soon as they are perceived, are classified according to their most evident similarities. This fact, which has nothing to do with any theory, is something that theory has to take account of. Realism does precisely that and in this respect is following common sense. That is why every form of realism is a philosophy of common sense.

11. It does not follow from this that common sense is a philosophy; but all sound philosophy presupposes common sense and trusts it, granted of course that, whenever necessary, appeal will be made from ill-informed to better-informed common sense. This is how science goes about things; science is not a critique of common sense but of the successive approximations to reality made by common sense. The history of science and philosophy witness to the fact that common sense, thanks to the methodical use it makes of its resources, is quite capable of invention. We should, therefore, ask it to keep criticizing its conclusions, which means asking it to remain itself, not to renounce itself.

12. The word "invention", like many others, has been contaminated by idealism. To invent means to *find*, not to *create*. The inventor resembles the creator only in the practical order, and especially in the production of artifacts, whether utilitarian or artistic. Like the scientist, the philosopher only invents by finding, by *discovering* what up to that point had been hidden. The activity of his intelligence, therefore, consists exclusively in the exercise of his *speculative* powers in regard to reality. If it creates anything, what it creates is never an object, but a way of explaining the object from within that object.

13.   This is also why the realist never expects his knowledge to engender an object without which his knowledge would not exist. Like the idealist, he uses his power of reflection, but keeping it within the limits of a reality given from without. Therefore the starting point of his reflections has to be being, which in effect is for us the beginning of knowledge: *res sunt*. If we go deeper into the nature of the object given us, we direct ourselves toward one of the sciences, which will be completed by a metaphysics of nature. If we go deeper into the conditions under which the object is given us, we shall be turning toward a psychology, which will reach completion in a metaphysics of knowledge. The two methods are not only compatible; they are complementary, because they rest on the primitive unity of the subject and object in the act of knowledge, and any complete philosophy implies an awareness of their unity.

14.   There is nothing, therefore, to stop the realist going, by way of reflective analysis, from the object as given in knowledge to the intellect and the knowing subject. Quite the contrary, this is the only way he has of assuring himself of the existence and nature of the knowing subject. *Res sunt, ergo cognosco, ergo sum res cognoscens.* [Things exist, therefore I know, therefore I am a knowing subject.] What distinguishes the realist from the idealist is not that one refuses to undertake this analysis whereas the other is willing to, but that the realist refuses to take the final term of his analysis for a principle generating the thing being analyzed. Because the analysis of knowledge leads us to the conclusion "I think", it does not follow that this "I think" is the first principle of knowledge. Because every representation is, in fact, a thought, it does not follow that it is only a thought, or that an "I think" conditions all my representations.

15. Idealism derives its whole strength from the consistency with which it develops the consequences of its initial error. One is, therefore, mistaken in trying to refute it by accusing it of not being logical enough. On the contrary, it is a doctrine which lives by logic, and only by logic, because in it the order and connection of ideas replaces the order and connection between things. The fatal leap (*saltus mortalis*) that catapults the doctrine into its consequences precedes the doctrine. Idealism can justify everything with its method except idealism itself, for the cause of idealism is not of idealist stamp; it does not even have anything to do with the theory of knowledge—it belongs to the moral order.

16. Preceding any philosophical attempt to explain knowledge is the fact, not only of knowledge itself, but of men's burning desire to understand. If reason is too often content with summary and incomplete explanations, if it sometimes does violence to the facts by distorting them or passing them over in silence when they are inconvenient, it is precisely because its passion to understand is stronger than its desire to know, or because the means of acquiring knowledge at its disposal are not powerful enough to satisfy it. The realist is just as much exposed to these temptations as the idealist, and yields to them just as frequently. The difference is that he yields to them against his principles, whereas the idealist makes it a principle that he can lawfully yield to them. Realism, therefore, starts with an acknowledgment by the intellect that it will remain dependent on a reality which causes its knowledge. Idealism owes its origin to the impatience of a reason which wants to reduce reality to knowledge so as to be sure that its knowledge lets none of reality escape.

17. The reason idealism has so often been in alliance with mathematics is that this science, whose object is quantity, extends its jurisdiction over the whole of material nature, insofar as material nature has to do with quantity. But while idealism may imagine that the triumphs of mathematics in some way justify it, those triumphs owe nothing to idealism. They are in no way bound up with it, and they justify it all the less, seeing that the most mathematically oriented physics conducts all its calculations within the ambit of the experimental facts that those calculations interpret. Someone discovers a new fact and what happens? After vain attempts to make it assimilable, all mathematical physics will reform itself so as to be able to assimilate it. The idealist is rarely a scientist, more rarely still a research scientist in a laboratory, and yet it is the laboratory that provides the material which tomorrow's mathematical physics will have to explain.

18. The realist, therefore, does not have to be afraid that the idealist may represent him as opposed to scientific thought, since every scientist, even if philosophically he thinks himself an idealist, in his capacity as a scientist thinks as a realist. A scientist never begins by defining the method of the science he is about to initiate. Indeed, the surest way of recognizing false sciences is by the fact that they make the method come first. The method, however, should derive from the science, not the science from the method. That is why no realist has ever written a *Discourse on the Method*. He cannot know how things are known before he knows them nor discover how to know each order of things except in knowing it.

19. The most dangerous of all the different methods is the "reflective method"; the realist is content with "reflection". When reflection becomes a method, it is no longer just an intelligently directed reflection, which it should be, but a reflection that substitutes itself for reality in that its principles and system become those of reality itself. When the "reflective method" remains faithful to its essence, it always assumes that the final term of its reflection is at the same time the first principle of our knowledge. As a natural consequence of this it follows that the last step in the analysis must contain virtually the whole of what is being analyzed; and, finally, that whatever cannot be discovered in the end point of the reflection, either does not exist or can legitimately be treated as not existing. This is how people are led into excluding from knowledge, and even from reality, what is necessary for the very existence of knowledge.

20. There is a second way of recognizing the false sciences generated by idealism; in starting from what they call thought, they are compelled to define truth as a special case of error. Taine did a great service for good sense when he defined sensation as a true hallucination, because he showed, as a result, where logic necessarily lands idealism. Sensation becomes what a hallucination is when this hallucination is not one. So we must not let ourselves be impressed by the famous "errors of the senses", nor startled by the tremendous business idealists make about them. Idealists are people for whom the normal can only be a particular instance of the pathological. When Descartes states triumphantly that even a madman cannot deny his first principle "I think, therefore I am", he helps us enormously to see what happens to reason when reduced to this first principle.

21. We must, therefore, regard the arguments about dreams, illusions, and madness, borrowed by idealists from skeptics, as errors of the same kind. The fact that there are visual illusions chiefly proves that all our visual perceptions are not illusions. A man who is dreaming feels no different from a man who is awake, but anyone who is awake knows that he is altogether different from someone who is dreaming; he also knows it is because he has had sensations, that he afterward has what are called hallucinations, just as he knows he would never dream about anything if he had not been awake first. The fact that certain madmen deny the existence of the outside world, or even (with all due respect to Descartes) their own, is no grounds for considering the certainty of our own existence as a special case of "true delirium". The idealist only finds these illusions so upsetting because he does not know how to prove they are illusions. The realist has no reason to be upset by them, since for him they really are illusions.

22. Certain idealists say that our theory of knowledge puts us in the position of claiming to be infallible. We should not take this objection seriously. We are simply philosophers for whom truth is normal and error abnormal; this does not mean it is any easier for us to reach the truth than it is to achieve and conserve perfect health. The realist differs from the idealist, not in being unable to make mistakes, but principally in that, when he does make mistakes, the cause of the error is not a thought which has been unfaithful to itself, but an act of knowledge which has been unfaithful to its object. But above all, the realist only makes mistakes when he is unfaithful to his principles, whereas the idealist is in the right only insofar as he is unfaithful to his.

23. When we say that all knowledge consists in grasping the thing as it is, we are by no means saying that the intellect infallibly so grasps it, but that only when it does grasp it as it is will there be knowledge. Still less do we mean that knowledge exhausts the content of its object in a single act. What knowledge grasps in the object is something real, but reality is inexhaustible, and even if the intellect had discerned all its details, it would still be confronted by the mystery of its very existence. The person who believed he could grasp the whole of reality infallibly and at one fell swoop was the idealist Descartes. Pascal, the realist, clearly recognized how naïve was the claim of philosophers that they could "comprehend the principles of things, and from there—with a presumption as infinite as their object—go on to knowing everything". The virtue proper to the realist is modesty about his knowledge, and even if he does not practice it, he is committed to it by his calling.

24.   A third way of recognizing the false sciences which idealism generates is by the fact that they feel it necessary to "ground" their objects. That is because they are not sure their objects exist. For the realist, whose thought is concerned with being, the good, the true, and the beautiful are in the fullest sense real, since they are simply being itself as desired, known, and admired. But as soon as thought substitutes itself for knowledge, these transcendentals begin to float in the air without knowing where to perch themselves. This is why idealism spends its time "grounding" morality, knowledge, and art, as though the way men should act were not written in the nature of man, the manner of knowing in the very structure of our intellect, and the arts in the practical activity of the artist himself. The realist never has to ground anything, but he has to discover the foundations of his operations, and it is always in the nature of things that he finds them: *operatio sequitur esse.*

25.   So we must carefully avoid all speculation about "values", because values are simply and solely transcendentals that have cut adrift from being and are trying to take its place. "The grounding of values" is the idealist's obsession; for the realist it is meaningless.

26.   The most painful thing for a man of our times is not to be taken for a "critical spirit". Nevertheless, the realist should resign himself to not being one, because the critical spirit is the cutting edge of idealism, and in this capacity it has the characteristics not of a principle or doctrine but of zeal for a cause. The critical spirit expresses, in effect, a determination to submit facts to whatever treatment is necessary so that nothing in them remains refractory to the mind. To achieve this, there is only one policy; everywhere the point of view of the observer must be substituted for that of the thing observed. The discrediting of reality will be pursued, if necessary, to its most extreme consequences, and the harder reality resists, the more determined the idealist will be to disregard it. The realist, on the other hand, should always recognize that the object is what causes knowledge and should treat it with the greatest respect.

27. Respecting the object of knowledge means, above all, a refusal to reduce it to something which complies with the rules of a type of knowledge arbitrarily chosen by ourselves. Introspection, for instance, does not allow us to reduce psychology to the level of an exact science. This, however, is not a reason for condemning introspection, for it seems probable that, the object of psychology being what it is, psychology ought not to be an exact science, not at least if it is to remain faithful to its object. Human psychology, such as a dog knows it, ought to be at least as conclusive as our science of nature, just as our science of nature is about as penetrating as human psychology as known by a dog. The psychology of behavior is therefore very wise to adopt the dog's outlook on man, because as soon as consciousness makes its appearance, it reveals so much to us that the infinite gulf between a science of consciousness and consciousness itself leaps to the eye. If our organism were self-conscious, who knows whether biology and physics would still be possible?

28. The realist must, therefore, always insist, against the idealist, that for every order of reality there is a corresponding way of approaching and explaining it. He will then find that, having refused to embark on a critique preliminary to knowledge, he is free—much freer than the idealist—to embark on a critique of the different branches of knowledge by measuring them against their object; for the "critical spirit" criticizes everything except itself, whereas the realist, because he is not a "critical spirit", is continuously self-critical. The realist will never believe that a psychology which in order to understand consciousness better starts by placing itself outside consciousness will give him the equivalent of consciousness; nor will he believe, with Durkheim, that the real savages are those found in books, or that social life consists essentially of prohibitions with sanctions attached, as though the only society we had to explain were the one described in Leviticus. Nor will he imagine that historical criticism is in a better position than the witnesses it invokes to determine what happened to them or discern the exact meaning of what they themselves said. That is why realism, in subordinating knowledge to its objects, places the intelligence in the most favorable position for making discoveries. For if it is true that things did not always happen exactly as their witnesses supposed, the relative errors they may have made are a trifling matter compared to those our imaginations will embroil us in if we start reconstructing facts, feelings, and ideas we never experienced, according to our own notions of what seems probable.

29. Such is the liberty of the realist. We can only choose between deferring to the facts and so being free in thought, or being free with the facts and the slave of thought. So let us turn to the things themselves that knowledge apprehends, and to the relationship between the different branches of knowledge and the things that they apprehend, so that, conforming itself ever more closely to them, philosophy can progress once more.

30. It is in this spirit, too, that we should read the great philosophers who have preceded us on the realist path. "It is not in Montaigne," wrote Pascal, "but in myself that I find everything I see within." And we can equally say here, "It is not in Saint Thomas or Aristotle, but in things, that the true realist sees everything he sees." So he will not hesitate to make use of these masters, whom he regards solely as guides toward reality itself. And if the idealist reproached him, as one of them has just had the kindness to do, with "decking himself out in hand-me-downs taken for truths", he will have his answer ready: much better to deck oneself out in truths that others have handed down, as the realist, when necessary, is willing to do, rather than, like the idealist, refuse to do so and go naked.

INDEX